▶ Football and the FA Women's Super League

DOI: 10.1057/9781137480323.0001

Other Palgrave Pivot titles

Domagoj Hruška: **Radical Decision Making: Leading Strategic Change in Complex Organizations**

Bjørn Møller: **Refugees, Prisoners and Camps: A Functional Analysis of the Phenomenon of Encampment**

Emily F. Henderson: **Gender Pedagogy: Teaching, Learning and Tracing Gender in Higher Education**

Mihail Evans: **The Singular Politics of Derrida and Baudrillard**

Bryan Fanning and Andreas Hess: **Sociology in Ireland: A Short History**

Tom Watson (editor): **Latin American and Caribbean Perspectives on the Development of Public Relations: Other Voices**

Anshu Saxena Arora and Sabine Bacouël-Jentjens (editors): **Advertising Confluence: Transitioning the World of Marketing Communications into Social Movements**

Bruno Grancelli: **The Architecture of Russian Markets: Organizational Responses to Institutional Change**

Michael A. Smith, Kevin Anderson, Chapman Rackaway, and Alexis Gatson: **State Voting Laws in America: Voting Fraud, or Fraudulent Voters?**

Nicole Lindstrom: **The Politics of Europeanization and Post-Socialist Transformations**

Madhvi Gupta and Pushkar: **Democracy, Civil Society, and Health in India**

George Pattison: **Paul Tillich's Philosophical Theology: A Fifty-Year Reappraisal**

Alistair Cole and Ian Stafford: **Devolution and Governance: Wales between Capacity and Constraint**

Kevin Dixon and Tom Gibbons: **The Impact of the 2012 Olympic and Paralympic Games: Diminishing Contrasts, Increasing Varieties**

Felicity Kelliher and Leana Reinl: **Green Innovation and Future Technology: Engaging Regional SMEs in the Green Economy**

Brian M. Mazanec and Bradley A. Thayer: **Deterring Cyber Warfare: Bolstering Strategic Stability in Cyberspace**

Amy Barnes, Garrett Wallace Brown and Sophie Harman: **Global Politics of Health Reform in Africa: Performance, Participation, and Policy**

Densil A. Williams: **Competing against Multinationals in Emerging Markets: Case Studies of SMEs in the Manufacturing Sector**

Nicos Trimikliniotis, Dimitris Parsanoglou and Vassilis S. Tsianos: **Mobile Commons, Migrant Digitalities and the Right to the City**

Claire Westall and Michael Gardiner: **The Public on the Public: The British Public as Trust, Reflexivity and Political Foreclosure**

Federico Caprotti: **Eco-Cities and the Transition to Low Carbon Economies**

DOI: 10.1057/9781137480323.0001

palgrave▶pivot

Football and the FA Women's Super League: Structure, Governance and Impact

Carrie Dunn
University of East London, UK

and

Joanna Welford
Loughborough University, UK

palgrave
macmillan

DOI: 10.1057/9781137480323.0001

First published 2015 by
PALGRAVE MACMILLAN

Palgrave Macmillan in the UK is an imprint of Macmillan Publishers Limited,
registered in England, company number 785998, of Houndmills, Basingstoke,
Hampshire RG21 6XS.

Palgrave Macmillan in the US is a division of St Martin's Press LLC,
175 Fifth Avenue, New York, NY 10010.

Palgrave Macmillan is the global academic imprint of the above companies
and has companies and representatives throughout the world.

Palgrave® and Macmillan® are registered trademarks in the United States,
the United Kingdom, Europe and other countries.

ISBN: 978-1-137-48033-0   EPUB
ISBN: 978-1-137-48032-3   PDF
ISBN: 978-1-137-48031-6   Hardback

A catalogue record for this book is available from the British Library.

A catalog record for this book is available from the Library of Congress.

www.palgrave.com/pivot

DOI: 10.1057/9781137480323

Contents

Acknowledgements

We would like to thank the people who have helpfully given their time to talk to us in the course of researching this book.

▶

DOI: 10.1057/9781137480323.0002

Author Biographies

Carrie Dunn is a journalist and academic who has been combining research, teaching and professional practice since 2005. She is the programme leader for sports journalism at the University of East London. Her research interests include fandom, sport, feminism and the consumption of popular culture, and her PhD examined the experience of the female football supporter in the English professional game. As a journalist, she divides her time between writing about sport and writing about popular culture, for publications including *The Times* and *The Guardian*.

Jo Welford is a research associate at Loughborough University in the School of Sport, Exercise and Health Sciences. She has spent the majority of her ten-year research career working in the area of gender and sport, with a particular interest in women's football. Her PhD investigated the structure of female football in the UK under the Football Association, before the formation of the Women's Super League. Jo has spent most of her life playing football, starting out as the only girl in a primary school team until she reached an age where this was no longer allowed. Combining playing and supporting the game with an academic interest has given her a critical insight into various aspects of women's football.

List of Abbreviations

BBC	British Broadcasting Corporation
BT	British Telecom
DCMS	Department for Culture, Media and Sport (UK)
DFB	Deutscher Fußball-Bund (German Football Federation)
ESPN	Entertainment and Sports Programming Network
EU	European Union
FA	The Football Association
FC	Football Club
FAWSL	The Football Association Women's Super League (also WSL)
FIFA	Fédération Internationale de Football Association (International Federation of Association Football)
GB	Great Britain
MP	Member of Parliament
OOH	Out of Home (marketing company)
PR	Public Relations
UEFA	Union of European Football Associations
USA	United States of America
WFA	Women's Football Association
WPL	Women's Premier League
WPS	Women's Professional Soccer League (USA)
WSC	*When Saturday Comes* (magazine)
WSFF	Women's Sport and Fitness Foundation
WSL	Women's Super League (also FAWSL)
WUSA	Women's United Soccer Association (USA)

DOI: 10.1057/9781137480323.0004

Introduction

Abstract: *This prefatory chapter introduces the current status of women's football in the UK and acknowledges its position in the wider European context, before giving an outline of the rest of the book.*

Dunn, Carrie and Joanna Welford. *Football and the FA Women's Super League: Structure, Governance and Impact*. Basingstoke: Palgrave Macmillan, 2015. DOI: 10.1057/9781137480323.0005.

▶

The referee blows his whistle at 3.50pm on Sunday 12 October 2014. The Liverpool players celebrate, albeit tentatively – as it stands, they have won the league title. But two other games are still in play, and a goal by either Birmingham or Chelsea will snatch the title. Neither side can manage a last gasp title-winner; the celebrations can now start for real as Liverpool retain the league trophy on goal difference. But this is not a moment of glory for Steven Gerrard. Liverpool Ladies captain Gemma Bonner lifts the trophy amid the streamers and champagne corks.

The 2014 season of the semi-professional FA Women's Super League (FAWSL) saw one of the tightest end-of-season battles that English football had ever seen. In its fourth season, this dramatic final day of the FAWSL suggested that it has succeeded in one of its primary aims of increasing the competitiveness of elite women's football. Further, the game was televised live on BT Sport; although this is a subscription channel, the final day title-decider was shown free-to-view, so was available to all. The 2014 season also saw an expansion to the original single-division closed FAWSL, with a second division extending the number of teams to 18. This is an important time for English women's football, a sport that has struggled to emerge from the shadows of its male counterpart. Since the start of the FAWSL in 2011, top female players can now receive a wage for playing football in England. Games are screened live on television. Spectator numbers are on the rise. And in 2014, the FA announced that England women would be playing an international match on the hallowed turf of Wembley Stadium – against Germany.

It would be easy to be swept away in the excitement that the FAWSL has created on behalf of women's football more widely. It has certainly generated an air of anticipation around the game that has rarely been seen before. But four years in, it is important to step back and critically reflect on the recent history of women's football and what the FAWSL has achieved (and just as significantly, what it has not achieved). What has been the impact of this new women's football league, which, with its closed model, licencing system and summer league season, is structurally alien to football in Europe?

We intend for this book to do just that. The year 2014 represents a crucial time in women's football: the FAWSL has had four years to find its feet, establish and develop its market, and look back on its original aims. Teething problems should have been ironed out, and the league by now should be settled in what it is and what it is trying to do. The expansion to two divisions represents the first major structural change,

DOI: 10.1057/9781137480323.0005

and it is important to also consider the impact of this. As the Football Association are yet to announce any long-term plans for the league, with funding only guaranteed until 2018, it is imperative that those inside and outside of the game critically reflect on the recent past, current and future role of the league. Europe more widely is also seeing an increase in the professionalisation of women's football – of players, clubs, leagues and competitions – but there has yet to be extensive critical reflection on these significant changes. We are not suggesting that professionalisation is purely a recent phenomenon, but inarguably this has increased in recent years and looks set to continue doing so. Many European leagues have seen moves towards professionalisation that are so recent it is impossible to judge their successes (or failures). However the struggles faced by the various women's leagues in the USA since WUSA, the world's first professional football (soccer) league for women, was launched in 2000 suggest that instability will likely continue to afflict any attempts to increase professionalisation of the sport. In a constantly changing field, it is imperative that changes are monitored, successes are evaluated and failures are exposed as women's football grows.

This book is a sociological analysis of the current state of women's football in England, investigating the significant structural changes that have shaped its recent history (and are likely to shape its future). It is broadly divided into two parts. The first part, Chapters 1 to 3, looks at how elite women's football has got to where it is in 2014. Publicly available information, such as FA documents and media reports, are collated and discussed alongside the most significant academic work in the area to contextualise the current structure and culture of the FAWSL. Chapter 1 gives a very brief introduction to the development of the game since its first recorded appearance at the end of the nineteenth century. The present is shaped by the past, and in nowhere is this more evident than women's football. From its early war-time boom, to its silenced years, to the takeover by the Football Association in 1993, women's football has had a turbulent relationship with the male structures that govern the game. There has been a consistent tension between discourses of participation and professionalisation, and the state of the game at the start of the twenty-first century reflected this. Women were playing the game in increasing numbers but continued to face discrimination and difficulties, on and off the field. It is in this context that the FAWSL was conceived, therefore it is important to understand the current (and potential future) status of women's football

DOI: 10.1057/9781137480323.0005

as embedded in and shaped by this contradictory context. Chapter 2 discusses the beginnings of the league itself, examining issues facing its launch in 2011 and reflecting on the inaugural season. This chapter closely examines the format of the league, particularly those features unique to football in England and those learnt from the successes and failures of women's professional soccer in the USA. The expansion to two divisions is the focus of Chapter 3, the only significant structural change to the league since its launch. Documents released around the time of the expansion refer to the successes of the FAWSL across its first three seasons; these are discussed in relation to the expansion and the future direction the league is being directed in.

The second part of the book, Chapters 4 to 6, move the discussion from the structural aspects of the league to the impact that the FAWSL has had. Here, we supplement available documentation and reports with our own empirical research. Chapter 4 examines two case studies that demonstrate the impact that the unique structural aspects of the FAWSL, particularly the licensing system, can have on clubs. Firstly, FAWSL club Doncaster Belles, with a long successful history in the sport, saw their application for the top league rejected, instead receiving a place in the newly formed FAWSL second division. Secondly, Lincoln Ladies did not apply for a 2014 FAWSL licence, instead applying as Notts County Ladies, which involved a radical overhaul to the club and a move to a different city. These two cases had a significant impact on various aspects of the game, a number of which are discussed in detail here. The media attention afforded to the FAWSL is the focus of Chapter 5. Women's sport, and football in particular, is notoriously under-represented in the media, and though women's participation in the sport has grown, this has not been reflected in an equal expansion of coverage. The thoughts of current FAWSL players are included to illustrate the difficulties faced by the sport and its participants but also the potential it has to attract and inspire young females to football. Media profiles play an important part in the commercial strategy of FAWSL clubs and the league more widely, so this is an aspect of women's football that has changed significantly with the addition of the new league. Chapter 6 builds on this in considering an oft-overlooked segment of sport – the fans. The FAWSL is aimed at a particular market, so it is useful to consider whether strategies to engage this target group have been successful or even reached beyond this.

Chapter 7 concludes the book by bringing the two parts together and looking to the future. In evaluating the success of the FAWSL in relation

DOI: 10.1057/9781137480323.0005

to its original aims, we critically reflect on the first four years of the league. The structure of the FAWSL is framing its impact, in particular those features that are experimental in English football. We argue that those features are creating as many difficulties as they are trying to overcome. The summer league season in particular is problematic for women's football, both culturally and structurally, despite being conceived to overcome potential issues. This chapter looks outside of the FAWSL when considering the impact of the league – there is an expansive pyramid below the FAWSL where the vast majority of female players experience football. Finally, we consider the future of the league and its format, particularly the major challenges it faces.

It is outside of the scope of this book to provide an in-depth historical account of the development of English women's football and the changing experience of players across this time. This has been done excellently elsewhere, and we would direct readers towards Jean Williams' (2003) detailed examination of how the sport has developed in England from its war-time boom through to the modern game at the start of the twenty-first century. Sue Lopez (1997) also presents an illuminating overview, particularly considering her own personal history as an elite player; and Gail Newsham (1994) and Tim Tate (2013) – among others – provide engaging accounts of female players and teams that were kicking a football around long before England (men) won the World Cup in 1966.

For a more global perspective, the collection of essays in Women, Soccer, and Sexual Liberation, edited by Hong and Mangan (2004), illustrate the development of football for women across the world and highlight not only past but also present and future struggles for legitimacy in different countries. The current situation of semi-professional women's football in England is, as we hope to illustrate, unique in many ways but at the same time also has parallels with other nations within and even outside of Europe. It is again beyond our scope to position the current English context within the wider world of women's football in any detail; however, we do not underestimate the importance of player migration, international competitions and the increased but still relatively minimal attention given to women's football by UEFA and FIFA in the global schematic of the game. Williams (2013) and Agergaard and Tielser (2014) explore some of these global issues and their implications for the women's game. This is a crucial time for women's football, and the struggle currently facing the top of the game in England is just one of many that continue to be fought globally.

DOI: 10.1057/9781137480323.0005

Although academic attention to the sport is growing, and several scholars have worked tirelessly to provide it with an accessible history, women's football remains an under-researched area. As the game continues to grow, so must this attention. The landscape of semi-professional and professional football for women globally is one of constant change and flux. Not a season goes by without reports of leagues launching or ceasing, expanding or depleting, or male–female club relationships solidifying or failing. Some leagues remain experimental, so will be reviewed by national federations who will judge their success and decide their futures. The English FAWSL is one of these leagues. It represents one of the biggest developments in the history of the sport, and we hope that this book provides a useful introduction and context to the first semi-professional women's football league in England.

DOI: 10.1057/9781137480323.0005

1

The FAWSL's Context within the History of Women's Football

Abstract: *This chapter gives a succinct overview of the development of the sport and the academic attention offered to women's football to the present date, highlighting how this has contributed to knowledge of and current debates surrounding the sport. It includes work on not just the UK context but what has been learnt from the development of women's football in Europe and North America. It provides a backdrop for our argument that an examination of the FAWSL can contribute to, extend and develop findings of previous research.*

Dunn, Carrie and Joanna Welford. *Football and the FA Women's Super League: Structure, Governance and Impact.* Basingstoke: Palgrave Macmillan, 2015. DOI: 10.1057/9781137480323.0006.

Introduction

'The future is feminine', declared Sepp Blatter, the General Secretary of the Fédération Internationale de Football Association (FIFA), in 1995 following a successful Women's World Cup in Sweden (cited in Williams, 2004: 114). It was also a time of optimism for women's football in the UK. The national governing body, the Football Association (FA), had recently taken over the organisational side of the women's game, bringing it under the umbrella of the male model of football governance and establishing a Women's Football Committee. Although few would agree with the current president of the world football governing body that the future of such a traditionally male sport was even verging on the feminine, there was perhaps at least a hint of optimism in the air. Women had fought long and hard to be given the opportunity not just to play football but also to be taken seriously as competitors, and the 1993 FA takeover was the signal from above that the game had been waiting for. In 2011, the FA launched the Women's Super League (WSL), the first semi-professional football league for women, marking the beginning of a new era for the sport.

The current state of women's football must, however, be understood as a product of the context in which it has developed. Football for women did not start with the FA takeover in 1993. Prior to this, the Women's Football Association (WFA) independently ran the sport for 24 years, and before that, more informal structures extend back to the late nineteenth century (Williams, 2007). The well-publicised recent growth in female participation in football as promoted by the FA since 1993 (see Table 1.1) tends to overshadow the formal and informal policies and practices that have excluded women from football, and encourages the perception that women's involvement in the sport is a recent

TABLE 1.1   *Registered female football players and teams, 1993–2003*

Season	Women's teams	Women players	Girl's teams	Girl players	Total players
1993	400	10400	80	800	11200
1996/97	500	13000	750	15000	28000
1997/98	600	15600	850	17000	32600
1998/99	650	16900	960	19200	36100
1999/2000	700	18200	1150	23000	41200
2000/01	741	19366	1800	36000	55500
2001/02	804	20000	2200	41667	61667
2002/03	865	21265	4820	63301	84926

DOI: 10.1057/9781137480323.0006

phenomenon – there is no central archive for women's football records (Williams, 2003). This not only demonstrates a lack of awareness of the challenges women have attempted to make to the male dominance of the sport but also denies women history and renders them invisible in the development of what is often termed England's 'National Game'.[1] Such is the lack of acknowledgement given to the role of women in nineteenth- and early-twentieth-century football, Tim Tate's (2013) examination of female football players in this period of history is aptly subtitled 'The Secret History of Women's Football'.

In an attempt to reposition women within the history of football, and provide a context within which to understand the current position of women in the sport, a number of writers have provided an insight into the development of women's football from both a structural and individual perspective (Lopez, 1997; Melling, 1999; Newsham, 1997; Tate, 2013; Williams, 2003, 2004, 2007; Williams & Woodhouse, 1991; Williamson, 1991), giving the sport a historical identity. An in-depth historical assessment of the development of the sport is beyond the scope of this book – and has been covered excellently elsewhere, particularly by the authors above – but an understanding of how this has shaped the identity of football for women provides a valuable lens through which to view the current state of the game. Behind all the gloss of the first semi-professional women's football league in England lies a historically turbulent relationship between women who wish to play football and the male-dominated authorities that govern the game.

Historical development

The movement of women into the 'time honoured male preserve' of football (Williamson, 1991: 72) has traditionally been resisted in the majority of football nations, and with particular strength in the UK. In 1894, a British Ladies Football Club was founded, and a crowd of around 7,000 is reported to have attended their first match under FA rules in 1895; to put this in context, the previous season's (men's) FA Cup Final and Amateur Cup final drew crowds of 37,000 and 3,500 respectively (Williams, 2007). It is thought that the FA took a rather ambivalent attitude to the very early involvement of women in football, which Jean Williams (2007) considers reflective of their apparent predicament: the FA did not want to oversee the women's game, but neither did they wish

DOI: 10.1057/9781137480323.0006

to allow it to continue outside of their governance. However, women first began playing football in large numbers around 20 years later during the First World War. Matches were played in front of thousands of paying spectators to raise money for war charities.

At a time where women found structural and ideological space within football, coupled with social and political progress made by women in the absence of men, the sport grew. Women proved that they could function perfectly well within the spheres that traditional stereotypes had denied them (Melling, 1999). At the same time, the charity focus allowed their participation to be perceived as evidence of patriotism rather than moral decadence (Pfister et al., 2002). Importantly, due to the suspension of male football, women were not competing with the established male game for the football audience – they were not perceived as serious footballers, and therefore did not pose a direct threat to the masculine hegemony of the sport (Williams & Woodhouse, 1991). Further, there was no attempt to replicate the structure of the male football league competitions, as games were organised in different areas of the country in response to fund-raising demand and economic potential (Williams, 2007). This cultural and structural separation from men's football seemed to create a space for women's football to flourish.

At the peak of its popularity, 53,000 people watched Dick, Kerr Ladies – inarguably the most successful women's team in the history of the sport (see Newsham, 1997) – beat St Helens at Goodison Park, the home of Everton FC, on Boxing Day 1920. However, in the years shortly following the end of WWI, 'normalisation' returned to both male football leagues and the sexual division of labour. By 1921, the charitable nature of women's football had begun to lose its legitimacy, leading to press calls for a return to normality in the gender order (Pfister et al., 2002). On 5 December 1921, the FA passed a unanimous resolution stating their opinion on the unsuitability of football for women, and ruling that clubs forbid women from playing on their grounds.[2]

Media reports at the time supported the ban, believing it to be reflective of the general sports-watching public who felt that football was not a sport for women (see Williams, 2007 for examples). There is little doubt that the football authorities saw the rise of women's football as a threat to the male game (Giulianotti, 1999). The ban highlighted a resistance to women's involvement within the structures of male football that has persistently impacted the development of the sport and remains a significant issue today: the struggles over legitimacy and

DOI: 10.1057/9781137480323.0006

equality that female footballers faced in 1921 have not been completely eradicated.

Women wishing to play football in other European countries faced similar struggles after the war. Charity matches between men and women in Sweden had just started to grow into more organised regular female matches when the 1921 FA ban in England was implemented. The Swedish media used this to support the feeling amongst 'male football experts' that 'football is no sport for ladies' (Hjelm & Olofsson, 2004). In France, women's football matches had grown in popularity by the 1920s, but saw a similar decline follow. Although there was no official ban on women playing, interest was so low by 1932 that the French governing body stopped organising the women's championship (Senaux, 2011). Warnings from doctors about the impact football might have on the female body coupled with a lack of grounds to play on contributed to this decline (Prudhomme-Poncet, 2007). In Germany, a country that would come to dominate European women's football, the first recorded women's team was forced to close in 1931 only a year after forming due to public outcry (Pfister, 2004). So England was not alone in cutting short any momentum women's football might have gained in the early nineteenth century, but as will be discussed, was long behind other countries when it came to addressing this exclusion.

There is historical evidence that teams continued to play several years following the 1921 ban, even in front of sizeable crowds, and Dick, Kerr Ladies toured the USA in 1922 where women had begun to play football in colleges (Williams, 2007). But the longer-term implications of the ban were disastrous for women's football. Without permission to play in existing grounds, crowds were limited and the spectacle lost. The sport was socially, culturally and economically marginalised (Williams, 2004), and without official recognition and support, the public's interest, trust and credibility also disappeared (Williamson, 1991): the period of popularity was over. The development of football as a male preserve was protected, strengthening discourses of female unsuitability for physical contact sports.

Despite this exclusion and separation, women's football continued independently. A total of 48 member clubs formed the Women's Football Association (WFA) in 1969. Women's football remained very much a participatory activity rather than a spectator sport (Williams, 2006); a distinction which remained throughout its growth and arguably still lingers today. The WFA had no official sanction from the male governing

DOI: 10.1057/9781137480323.0006

body; although the FA altered the constitution allowing ladies' teams *permission to apply* for affiliation, the WFA found their requests for formal links with the FA rejected in 1971, 50 years after the original ban (Williams, 2007). Although UEFA affiliates had voted that very same year to recommend all member states to take control of women's football under their respective governing bodies, the English FA continued to resist this. FIFA were similarly reluctant to relax their regulations; Williams (2007) details correspondence between the WFA and the FA concerning a Women's World Cup proposal, to be hosted by England and supported by (male) World Cup winners including Bobby Moore, in which the FA merely reiterated FIFA's stance on sanctioning competitions for non-affiliate members: it would not happen. Ten years later, the 1981 FIFA technical meeting discussed the development of women's football in member states; despite reiterating its lack of desire to sanction a Women's World Cup, members did agree that the women's game should come under the jurisdiction of governing bodies – although this should be kept separate to women's football in case they should benefit from (male) coaching and training facilities (cited in Williams, 2007: 144).

So 80 years after the FA banned women from using football grounds, and only 30 years before the FA launched the WSL, FIFA reiterated the fear that women might benefit from the use of facilities clearly (and bizarrely) intended for the sole use of male players. The WFA continued to grow, although tensions over the direction the women's game should take were central throughout the history of the organisation with ideals of participation conflicting with a more competitive, professional approach (Williams and Woodhouse, 1991).

The FA takeover and beyond

In 1993, the FA formally took control of the administration of women's football from the WFA. As a voluntary organisation, the WFA had encountered problems in attempting to accommodate the growth of the sport, with a weak infrastructure compounded by financial difficulties (Lopez, 1997). To highlight the relative timing of this takeover, women were accommodated in their respective governing bodies in Germany, Norway, Denmark and Sweden in the early 1970s, following the UEFA call for national football associations to take responsibility for the women's game (Hjelm & Olofsson 2004; Fasting, 2004; Skille, 2008).

DOI: 10.1057/9781137480323.0006

Interestingly, the DFB (German Football Federation) accepted women's football in 1970 but modified the structure with shorter matches, no studs to be worn and matches played in the *summer months* instead of the winter (Pfister, 2004). (The FAWSL is played in the summer, a format with several unintended consequences that will be discussed throughout the rest of this book. The DFB clearly thought a summer season was more appropriate for what was a 'watered down' version of men's football.)

Post-1993, women's football began to be brought in line with the established male structure. Leagues and cups were given FA titles, a Women's Football Committee was established and the post of Women's Football Co-ordinator created. The league pyramid became more streamlined to match more closely the existing male football league pyramid. The FA proposed a professional league for women that would be in place by 2003. Hope Powell was appointed as the first full-time women's national football coach and 20 Centres of Excellence were set up throughout the country in 1998 to provide a pathway for talented girls. In the decade following the FA takeover, female participation figures in England, especially for girls, saw a rapid rise (Table 1.1) and in 2002 football overtook netball as the most popular sport for girls (Williams, 2013).

However, the majority of the changes that were made over the ten years following the FA takeover did little to alter the way female football was perceived – as an inferior version of real (male) football. There were serious concerns that women's football was simply being 'bolted on' to existing male structures, with little structural change to reflect the needs of women and girls (Sue Lopez, evidence submitted to DCMS, 2006). The proposed professional league did not materialise, and the FA remained a male-dominated institution. A recurring pattern from the 1920s to the present day is the lack of female influence in the decision-making structures of football, which creates a conflict of interest between female participants and male administrators. Integration of women's and men's football has involved the acceptance of an institution that historically dismissed the sport and has been traditionally hostile (at best) to the involvement of women (Williams, 2003). The 1993 takeover had a minimal impact on the male-dominated nature of the FA or the way female football was perceived (Williams, 2004). Despite repeated recommendations that the FA reform at the top level to reflect the increasingly 'diverse interests', little has changed in this regard to the present day (DCMS, 2006, 2011, 2013).

DOI: 10.1057/9781137480323.0006

Academic research since the 1993 takeover has provided a valuable critique of the impact that this had on the game. The FA has been criticised for its reluctant and limited acceptance of women into its organisational structures (Welford, 2008, 2011; Williams, 2003, 2004). Studies have demonstrated how although participation rates particularly amongst girls did indeed rise, they continued to face considerable opposition and a lack of both formal and informal opportunities (Griggs, 2004; Griggs & Biscomb, 2010; Jeanes & Kay, 2007; Harris, 2002; Skelton, 2000). Things were no better for adult recreational players who continued to negotiate the complex relationship between a traditionally male sport and constructions of femininity and sexuality (Caudwell, 1999, 2003, 2004; Harris, 2001, 2007; Scraton et al., 1999; Welford & Kay, 2007) and ethnicity (Scraton et al., 2005). The reported rise in football participation levels amongst girls and women, alongside the potential legitimacy given to women's football by being administered and co-ordinated by the FA, was seemingly doing little to break down the barriers to integration that women have historically faced.

Twelve years after the FA had taken over the running of women's football, the hosting of the European Women's Championships in England in 2005 gave the game a timely boost in profile. The FA considered the tournament a huge success, with 29,092 watching England's opening game against Finland (Bell and Blakey, 2010) and higher than expected audiences both in the stadium and for televised matches (Harlow, 2005). The Women's Sport Foundation went so far as to describe the televising of England matches at Euro 2005 as a 'real breakthrough' (cited in DCMS, 2006). This was a significant boost to the profile of the game and suggested an appetite for women's football amongst the public that might herald a new era of more equitable treatment of women's football (Bell, 2012). England's performance did not, however, match the anticipation and they finished disappointingly bottom of their group.

The on-field difficulties faced by the English national team at Euro 2005 were inarguably linked to the lack of competition at elite club level. By 2005, since first winning the Women's Premier League (WPL) in 1995, Arsenal had won the league title five years out of ten, and also the Women's FA Cup the same number of times. Other winners highlighted the London-centric nature of the elite level – other victors of the cup and league in the 1995–2005 period were Croydon, Fulham, Charlton and Millwall, with Everton's title win in 1998 bringing them the honour of being the only non-London based winners of the WPL, WFA Cup or

DOI: 10.1057/9781137480323.0006

League Cup over those ten years. In the following years, Arsenal would solidify their dominance by winning the league and cup double for each of the subsequent four seasons, giving them a total of nine WPL titles and six WFA Cup wins of a possible ten. Domestically, women's football in England was fast becoming a one-horse race, unappealing to fans and potential sponsors and not providing the competitive quality needed for the elite players to progress.

The state of women's football in the 2000s provides an important backdrop to the launch of the FAWSL in 2011. Rapidly increasing participation levels sat uncomfortably alongside very real struggles faced by women and girls wishing to play football. Attitudes around women in sport – particularly traditionally male sports such as football – continued to reflect dominant gendered discourses of appropriate female behaviour. More and more players, a healthy participation base at junior level, including much improved formal opportunities at school, and increased visibility of the top level of the sport were having little effect on this. Undoubtedly, deep-rooted cultural attitudes are incredibly difficult to shift, and changes in this respect were not expected overnight. This lack of progress in the early days of FA governance was the context in which the FAWSL was conceived.

Conclusion

Women have a long and turbulent history of playing football in England. From a war-time boom in players and spectators, the FA ban on women playing on football grounds effectively silenced the sport and curtailed any support it had received up to that point. The FA took over the running of women's football 72 years later, but problems that have plagued the game throughout its development did not change overnight – women who wished to play football continued to be marginalised, pressured to conform to gender roles and struggled to be accepted as anything near as equals in the football world. The situation that the sport had reached in the mid-2000s was summed up in the first detailed House of Commons report on women and football, where references were made to the need for significant reform of the elite level of the sport (DCMS, 2006). The report complimented the work of the FA since 1993 and referenced the growth in popularity of football amongst girls, but conceded that the game remained hindered by barriers 'rooted in cultural attitudes' (p.3).

DOI: 10.1057/9781137480323.0006

The report made a number of recommendations for improvements at all levels of the sport, stressing that the situation at the time remained far from equitable. However, it was the recommendations for reform at the elite level that led to the greatest change.

The DCMS (2006) report criticised the WPL as being unstable, stating that the FA had acknowledged a 'severe imbalance' in the league. Recommendation 12 stated that a women's summer league was 'a promising way forward' (p.16). The Women's Super League (WSL), which the FA suggested would raise the quality of competition, maximise revenues through sponsorship, gate receipts and media rights and enhance the visibility of role models, was clearly supported by the enquiry but not, as the FA proposed, if resourced from public funding. It was stressed that the FA should fund the league as a financial commitment reflecting the supposed priority assigned to women's football. The FA was being told in no uncertain terms to put its money where its mouth is, and from this, the first semi-professional football league for women in England started to finally become a reality.

Notes

1   The dominant position football holds in England, and Britain more widely, is reflected both in the overall visibility of the game, particularly in the sports media (see, for example, Harris, 1999) and the cultural dominance of the sport (see, for example, Sugden & Tomlinson, 1994). Further, in a recent structural review of the FA by Lord Burns (The FA, 2005), the two main components of the sport were frequently referred to in the terms 'professional game' and 'National Game' (caps in original), with the latter representing the amateur and semi-professional levels of the sport. This labelling is interpreted to infer the claim by the FA that the sport of football, as played by the majority of participants (non-professional), is the 'National Game' of England.

2   The official line adopted for this resolution was a lack of clarity concerning how revenues from games were used, suggesting that women were paid (Pfister et al., 2002). However there was no proof that underhand dealings ever took place (Williamson, 1991), and any confusion over figures not adding up was more likely a result of loose accounting procedures rather than corruption (Williams & Woodhouse, 1991). Researchers (for example Giulianotti (1999)) have commented that the ban was more likely a result of the significant popularity of women's football.

DOI: 10.1057/9781137480323.0006

2
The Launch of the FAWSL

Abstract: *Despite the historically turbulent relationship between women's football and the FA, culminating with a takeover in 1993 (20 years after FIFA recommended member states take responsibility for women's football), in 2011 the FA funded, implemented and promoted the first semi-professional football league for women. This chapter looks at the context within which the FA Women's Super League was developed, promoted and launched, and the way it was organised. The WSL represents an ambiguous concept in women's football – the move to professionalisation, whilst offering potential benefit to players and clubs, represents an engagement with the very structure of football that has traditionally rejected and suppressed the involvement of women at all levels. The unique structural aspects of the FAWSL are given particular consideration.*

Dunn, Carrie and Joanna Welford. *Football and the FA Women's Super League: Structure, Governance and Impact.* Basingstoke: Palgrave Macmillan, 2015. DOI: 10.1057/9781137480323.0007.

Introduction

The previous chapter discussed the growth of women's football from the early twentieth century through to the mid-2000s, the time in which the FAWSL was conceived and planned. Not for the first time in its history, women's football found itself struggling between discourses of participation and elitism, increasingly integrated into male football structures but facing continued resistance. The game was growing, certainly in terms of participation, but this growth was not being matched with an increase in profile. This chapter focuses on how the launch of the FAWSL, the biggest overhaul the game would face since the FA takeover, would attempt to address this.

A semi-professional football league for women moves closer

The 2006 DCMS report into women's football strongly recommended that the game be reformed at the elite level, to make it more competitive and increase the quality of play. The following year the FA were criticised for a lack of urgency with respect to developing women's football in response to the 2006 report (Leighton, 2007b). But plans for a semi-professional summer league did continue to develop over the next two years, and it was the release of the FA Women's Football Strategy (The FA, 2008) that finally detailed the proposition. This came on the back of a highly praised performance at a major tournament by the national team, who were knocked out in the quarter-finals of the 2007 World Cup by reigning champions, the USA. Subtitled 'Championing Growth and Excellence', the 2008 strategy document outlined a four-year plan for developing the women's game to grow and sustain participation at all levels alongside increasing the quality at the elite level. One of the goals in the document was to create an elite summer league for women.

The FA, fully responsible for the national team and the league structures, saw that an improvement in the national side would only be possible with a higher-quality domestic league with the best English players. This was in response to the increasing trend for the top English players moving abroad for full-time professional football – in 2009/10, seven English national players were playing in the Women's Professional Soccer League in the USA (Williams, 2013). The year 2009 saw central

DOI: 10.1057/9781137480323.0007

contracts provided to the top 17 players in the national side, paid by the FA and initially set at £16,000 a year, giving players the opportunity to spend more time training (The FA, 2008). Players must be home-based (affiliated to their local English county FA) to be offered a central contract (Williams, 2013), an attempt to keep the top national players playing domestically in England.

But it was the intended semi-professional Super League that would ultimately retain current and emerging English players. In September 2008, the FA finally announced that an eight-team Women's Super League would be launched in the summer of 2010. Except that it wasn't. Documents pertaining to the original 2010 launch, including a promotional brochure produced in February 2009, are now unavailable publicly. In March 2009, three weeks before the application deadline, it was announced that the league would be delayed until 2011.[1] The WPS, the second incarnation of the professional women's league in the USA (discussed further later), was due to start in 2009. If the WSL could launch in England in 2010, English players might stay and play in the WSL rather than be tempted to the USA (Dunmore, 2009). Whether the FA felt pressure to compete with the WPS is speculation, but the 2010 launch was delayed, justified by the FA as part of their cost-cutting (Leighton, 2009a). Clubs were encouraged to 'put their applications on hold until further notice'.[2]

The delay was widely criticised as shambolic and reflective of the low status of women's football in the eyes of the FA (Leighton, 2009a; Oatley, 2009), with England striker Lianne Sanderson blaming the delay for her move to the USA the following summer (Leighton, 2010a). The FA Chairman at the time, Lord Triesman, sent apologetic letters to all clubs but fear over the future of the league remained. Continued financial instability meant that he could not guarantee that the league would actually launch in 2011.[3] It seemed that the 2008 claim by the FA that women's football was a priority was being severely tested.

It came as some surprise then that later that year, the FA announced that the Women's Super League would indeed launch in 2011, and that applications were once again open (The FA, 2009a). Only six months had passed since Lord Triesman had confirmed that there were turbulent times ahead for the organisation, but whatever had happened in that time, the WSL was back on the table. New FA CEO Ian Watmore echoed claims from the previous year in suggesting that the 'time had arrived' for women's football (The FA, 2009a). Earlier in the year England had

DOI: 10.1057/9781137480323.0007

put in their best performance at a major tournament, losing in the final of the 2009 European Championships to Germany, a catalyst to build on according to Watmore (quoted in Leighton, 2009b). A revised Super League brochure was released, entitled 'Be Part of Football's Future' (The FA, 2009a), with an opening paragraph that pushed the now or never agenda and belied the turmoil that the elite level of the game was thrown into earlier that same year.

Learning lessons from the USA

Before looking in more detail at the launch brochure and the intended format, aims and objectives of the FAWSL, it is important to consider the recent history of professional football (soccer) in the USA. This is particularly useful as the FA discussed in various documents around this time how they were keen to 'learn lessons' from the situation in the USA, in adapting the more successful aspects of the US leagues whilst trying to avoid making the same mistakes (The FA, 2010). This is perhaps admirable, although it is difficult to compare the USA with any other contexts due to the unique features of how the sport has developed there (see, for example, Martinez, 2008).

Football (soccer) for women is hugely popular in the USA, particularly at the grassroots level, and a strong collegiate system drives this in part thanks to Title IX[4] ensuring equal funding to men's and women's programmes. Although it is easy to credit this legislation with the popularity of female soccer, the game also benefits from a lack of competition from men's soccer and a strong co-educational (mixed) model throughout (Williams, 2007). The continued rise in popularity of the sport in the USA culminated in the unprecedented success of the 1999 Women's World Cup, where more than 90,000 people watched the national team beat China on penalties in the final. Following the tournament, the USA players became media stars. The success of the World Cup was to be the springboard for the launch of the first US professional women's soccer league, and perhaps the most high-profile football league for women ever (Williams, 2013), the Women's United Soccer Association (WUSA) in 2001. But the league did not meet commercial expectations and could not be sustained financially, which saw it suspended after only three seasons reporting losses of $100 million (King, 2009). This failure was read as a lack of viability of women's football globally (Williams, 2013).

DOI: 10.1057/9781137480323.0007

If a professional football league for women could not be sustained in the USA, launched at the height of the sport's popularity in the country with the biggest grassroots participation base, what chance did it have of succeeding elsewhere?

It is then perhaps understandable that the FA was tentative about its claims and aspirations for the WSL, and took care to learn from the WUSA experience. The use of social media, website interaction and content and commercial partnerships were aspects that the FA took on board (The FA, 2010) – WUSA players worked hard to connect with fans, the target audience is grassroots and the product is differentiated from the male competition to appeal to certain sponsors (Williams, 2007). For the second attempt at a pro league in the USA, the Women's Professional Soccer (WPS) league launched in 2009 with smaller budgets, capped salaries and viewing figures in the stadium and on TV were not overstated – overall, ambitions were more modest (King, 2009). As this chapter will discuss, many of these features were to find their way into the FAWSL plans. Unfortunately, the WPS would also fail to succeed in the crowded US sports market, but that was not to be known as the FA were planning the WSL.

Planning the FAWSL

The 2009 FAWSL launch brochure outlined the objectives and format of the league, its financial structure and requirements, the competitive element (which strangely required a section of its own), the application process and a final deadlines and logistics section. Apart from the withdrawn predecessor to this document, there was no official material available giving details of the FAWSL before this was released, just references to an elite summer league in the Women's Football Strategy (The FA, 2008) and periodical statements on the FA website that made it into press releases. The 2009 launch document demonstrated what the FA were trying to do with women's football, and how and why they were planning to go about it.

Objectives

Although the FA had criticised the poor quality of the existing elite league, in this document it was celebrated as part of an overall 'cohesive

DOI: 10.1057/9781137480323.0007

structure' that encouraged players to 'develop to their full potential'. Many of the objectives have already been discussed in this chapter: to retain the most talented players, to create more paid opportunities in football for players, to support and strengthen the commercial viability and sustainability of the game. Two further aims are interesting. One is to improve the playing facilities for women. There is no doubt that women suffer from priority issues with facilities, particularly if they are linked to a male club, often coming below even male junior teams in the ranking (Williams, 2003; Welford, 2013). The scheduling of women's football on a Sunday afternoon means that there are often up to three fixtures a weekend before the women get their turn on the pitch, by which point (in winter especially) it is reduced to an either playable or unplayable boggy mess (Welford, 2008).

The final objective listed in the document is to 'strengthen the player pathway and playing base of the sport'. This is clearly not something that the FAWSL can achieve, as it is reliant on structures further down the pyramid – and even interaction between the levels, which is not possible for the closed league – but no further detail is given in this document on how this might work in reality.

Format

The FAWSL would run in the summer months. The justification for this is given as twofold: to give the league the best chance of succeeding commercially in having little competition from elsewhere in football and to help players prepare for international tournaments. The former reason makes sense; one of the major hurdles to women's football development across its history has been competition (that it could never expect to win) with men's football for resources, supporters, media space and attention (Williams, 2003; 2004). The latter makes less sense. Whilst a high-quality domestic league may improve the playing quality of England players, which has the potential to translate into the performance of the national team (although the English Premier League and the English men's football team question this theory), the point the FA make is that a summer league fits better with the international cycle – a questionable claim at best, as international tournaments will come mid-season for FAWSL players.

As with all previous reports of the league, it is described as 'semi-professional' – most players receive some financial remuneration but not

DOI: 10.1057/9781137480323.0007

enough to live off. At the time of the 2009 launch document, 17 England international players had just begun central contracts with the FA worth £16,000 a year. These are very much a 'freedom to train' contract rather than a wage that would represent full professionalisation (Williams, 2013). Clubs are also bound to a salary cap of £20,000 per player with the allowance of up to four players per club to receive a wage exceeding this, designed to spread the talent across the FAWSL clubs and maintain a healthy competitive balance. Modest salaries represent the need for a conservative approach to the elite league development, considered key to sustainability and learning from financial difficulties that have blighted both of the US professional women's leagues (Kessel, 2010). Although the FA will provide £12,000 to each club to part-fund ambassadorial roles – which is to be split over three individuals given a maximum of £4,000 each – FAWSL regulations state that clubs must fund any player wages, as any monies received from the FA are to be spent on other running costs. Anything close to £20,000 per player is clearly going to require significant financing from the club, and is therefore unlikely to be a reality for those clubs not associated with a 'Premier League giant' (Conn, 2011).

The league would be limited to an 'optimum' of eight clubs, so as not to saturate the talent and provide as competitive a league as possible (The FA, 2010). Hope Powell believed this 'less is more' strategy would prioritise talent so as to best benefit the England squad (Williams, 2013). Despite the difference in season timings, FAWSL clubs would still play in the FA Cup, joining the last 16 in March – before the start of their season (The FA, 2009b).

Licensing

One of the main defining features of the FAWSL, and the one that separates it from the vast majority of football leagues in Europe, is the nature of the club licensing system. For the inaugural 2011 season, clubs had to apply for a place in the FAWSL. In reality the application criterion has no prerequisite of previous achievements or playing level, a fact that was made overt in the suggestion that applications from newly created clubs were welcome (The FA, 2009b). Clubs had to meet minimum requirements in four areas: financial and business management, commercial and marketing, facilities and playing and support staff. Successful clubs were guaranteed two years in the FAWSL

DOI: 10.1057/9781137480323.0007

(although this did in fact turn into three years), as there would be no relegation or changes to the league during this time – another feature in complete opposition to the traditional pyramid model of European football. The licensing model and its implications for clubs, players and the rest of the women's football pyramid are discussed in more detail in Chapters 4 and 7.

Branding

The FAWSL was very much built around a brand with a unique selling point designed to help make it sustainable. There is a clear drive to make women's football a family sport, and building a profile that appeals to this group is intended to make it a commercially attractive product in the long term (WSFF, 2009). Lessons learnt from the USA (The FA, 2010) include the accessibility of players – in sharp contrast to male footballers – with each club's 'digital ambassador' taking main responsibility for interacting with the fan base, with social media strategies featuring heavily in their work. Marketing strategies were designed around making the FAWSL appeal to families, with a key target audience being girls aged 9 to 15 (Williams, 2013). Focus groups were conducted in the early planning days with this target group, and the logo and strategy reflects their opinion that the brand should not be too 'girly' or 'fluffy'. All clubs have the same website format, built into the WSL overall site, to maintain the consistency of the brand.

Media coverage

Securing WSL broadcasting rights was a major goal for the FA to try to raise the profile and change perceptions of the game (The FA, 2008); one reason cited for the delay in the launch of the FAWSL was the collapse of TV company and FA media partner Setanta (Leighton, 2009b). Coverage of the European Championships in 2005 had been good with healthy viewing figures, but outside of those major tournaments, women's football, even at the elite level, was practically invisible. A deal was made with ESPN (a paid subscription channel) to show a weekly highlights programme and six live matches in the first season, representing a focus on quality rather than quantity (WSFF, 2009). The gulf between men's and women's football is underlined in this respect – ESPN would not pay for the rights, but would cover all production costs, considered a good deal in women's sports (Conn, 2011). Clubs also needed to outline their own strategy for developing and enhancing media relations in their application.

Sixteen teams applied for FAWSL licences: Arsenal, Barnet, Birmingham City, Bristol Academy, Chelsea, Colchester United, Doncaster Rovers Belles, Everton, Leeds Carnegie, Leicester City, Lincoln Ladies, Liverpool, Millwall Lionesses, Newcastle United, Nottingham Forest and Sunderland. Leeds Carnegie later withdrew their application after their university patrons were unable to commit to the finances required. (Their relationship with men's professional club Leeds United had ended with the withdrawal of funding in 2005.) Nine of the sixteen were from the current WPL, although Nottingham Forest and Bristol Academy finished in the relegation places at the end of the 2010 season. The remaining two WPL teams who did not submit applications were Blackburn Rovers, who could not get the financial support required by the men's club (Leighton, 2011c), and Watford, who did successfully apply for a 2014 FAWSL2 place following the expansion (discussed in the following chapter). Outside of the nine WPL applicants, the rest came from the second tier of the league, the WPL North or South. No 'new' clubs applied.

In March 2010, clubs were notified of the outcome of their applications. Arsenal, Birmingham City, Bristol Academy, Chelsea, Doncaster Rovers Belles, Everton, Lincoln Ladies and Liverpool were the eight successful clubs, six of which came from the existing top tier (WPL) and two from the existing second tier (WPL North and WPL South) (see Table 2.1). Lincoln was perhaps the 'surprise' inclusion, most probably due to their male professional club playing non-league football and the failed application of close neighbours and existing WPL team Nottingham Forest (Leighton, 2010b). Licences were originally awarded for two seasons, but these were automatically renewed for a third in 2012 whilst the FA considered how best to deal with the planned expansion beyond the eight teams.

April 2011: The FAWSL inaugural season starts

On 13 April 2011, the opening match of the FAWSL saw Chelsea host Arsenal at Imperial Fields, the home ground of Ryman Premier League (the seventh tier of the men's football pyramid) Tooting & Mitcham. The other three fixtures were held later the same evening. The 5.30 match

DOI: 10.1057/9781137480323.0007

TABLE 2.1   *Applications received for the 2011 FAWSL (successful applicants shaded)*

Applicant	2009–2010 league and position	
	First tier	Second tier
Arsenal	WPL, 1st	
Barnet		WPL South, 1st
Birmingham City	WPL, 10th	
Bristol Academy	WPL, 12th (relegation place)	
Chelsea	WPL, 3rd	
Colchester United		WPL South, 9th
Doncaster Rovers Belles	WPL, 6th	
Everton	WPL, 2nd	
Leeds Carnegie (withdrawn)	WPL, 4th	
Leicester City		WPL North, 3rd
Lincoln Ladies		WPL North, 2nd
Liverpool		WPL North, 1st
Millwall Lionesses	WPL, 8th	
Newcastle United		WPL North, 8th
Nottingham Forest	WPL, 11th (relegation place)	
Sunderland	WPL, 5th	

was screened live on ESPN, featuring entertainment in the form of bouncy castles, balloons and girl band Parade, with 2,510 paying spectators (Ronay, 2011). This followed an 'official' launch of the FAWSL at Wembley Stadium two days earlier, described by FA chairman David Bernstein as a 'true landmark' in women's football.[5] The entertainment aspect of FAWSL matches is considered important to the 'niche' nature of the brand, in providing a different experience from men's football.

Despite the opening evening of the FAWSL clashing with the men's UEFA Champions League quarter-finals – the summer league format intends to avoid competition with men's football, but April is a particularly busy time of the season – the first game was reported by many media outlets, launching the league with a 'fanfare' (WSFF, 2011). However some teething problems were reported, most notably the poor quality of the pitch (Ronay, 2011), questioning one of the goals of the FAWSL (to increase the quality of facilities for women to play on) from day one. Whilst a summer league might reduce competition for pitches, they are often not used over the summer for a very good reason – they are dry and well-used by this point of the year (BBC Sport, 2011). Players were also described as 'rusty' (Ronay, 2011), having not played a league match since the end of the WPL 2009–2010 season 11 months previously.

DOI: 10.1057/9781137480323.0007

The move to a summer league created an inevitably long break for the top teams between seasons, which was a clear frustration for players – almost all interviewed at the April 11th official launch stressed how keen they were to play again after such a long break.

No sooner had the season started, but it stopped again – a scheduled nine-week break for the Women's World Cup in Germany. To enable a break of such length, the first half of the 2011 season was squeezed into four weeks, which meant a frantic two games a week followed the April launch. Arsenal manager Laura Harvey described their opening two weeks of the season as 'crazy' with two WSL games, a Champions League home tie and an FA Cup semi-final to be played (cited in Leighton, 2011b). The summer league format requires a break every two years for the major international tournament – with the Olympics in 2012 also required a break – so delays in the first three seasons made it difficult for the league programme to gain and maintain any momentum. Hope Powell, then England manager, did believe that the first FAWSL season had delivered the most competitive women's football ever seen in England, which could only be of benefit to their World Cup preparations (cited in Leighton, 2011d). Five of the senior squad still, however, played their football in the USA.

Reflecting on the first FAWSL season

Follow-up documents from the FA and the Women's Sport and Fitness Foundation celebrated the successes of the first FAWSL season (The FA, 2012c; The FA, 2013a; The FAWSL, 2013; WSFF, 2011). The FA felt that the WSL had delivered four significant benefits, although these differed slightly from the objectives in the original 2009 launch brochure: a rise in playing standards, an improvement in playing and other career opportunities, growth in the profile of the game including media coverage and an uplift in commercial investment (The FA, 2013a). Playing standards are difficult to judge objectively, but the league was decided on the last day, which was considered a success in terms of competitiveness.

The growth in the profile of the game was believed to be a major success, expressed on a number of fronts: a 604% increase in top-flight attendances, higher than anticipated viewing figures for televised live matches (on a par with the Scottish Premier League[6]), increased awareness of the game and the FAWSL product, visible and accessible female

DOI: 10.1057/9781137480323.0007

role models, and significant social media interactions, all amounting to the development of a new fan base (The FA, 2012c). This is supported by the commercial benefits, such as securing contracts with major partners, their investment in the game at different levels and increasing interest from media and other commercial organisations. It is likely that all of these were helped by a successful Women's World Cup and a valiant effort from the English national team (although nowhere near the help that hosting the Olympics the following year would).

But there was little recognition from outside of this league that the rest of the pyramid had seen any benefits. Some clubs whose applications for a FAWSL place failed saw their top players move to clubs that offered top-level football and the chance to be a part of a semi-professional league. Three of the four Women's Premier League clubs who were not involved in the first FAWSL season experienced significant off-field problems that threatened the future of their club, with Blackburn Rovers, Leeds Carnegie and Nottingham Forest all struggling to survive after effectively being demoted to the second tier of the game.[7] The following winter season brought further instability for WPL clubs, as when they kicked off in August 2011 no decision had been made as to whether the FAWSL would see its planned expansion – and if that expansion would involve the WPL winners – following its second season. Sunderland, who saw their 2011 FAWSL application rejected and won the WPL the following two seasons, were unsurprisingly concerned about this lack of foresight by the FA (Leighton, 2011e). The rest of the women's football pyramid – which accounted for all but eight clubs – struggled to see how the changes at the top of the game were going to be of benefit to everyone else.

To bring this chapter around full circle, we return to the issue of whether the FA and the WSL can even begin to reconcile the difficulties faced by women in the sport more widely, despite their increasing participation: a position that has been referred to as 'outsiders on the inside' (Crosset, 1995; Welford, 2008). This term implies that liberal gains in terms of increased opportunities and the growth of game have not served as the basis of a more far-reaching change to the provision and perception of football for women or to the structures of football (Williams, 2003). Women are increasingly moving 'inside' football – not just as players, but as coaches, administrators, managers, fans and so on – but the football world remains male-dominated. Women's involvement in football falls short of integration. This is returned to in Chapter

DOI: 10.1057/9781137480323.0007

7, but for now, two incidents in 2011 demonstrate just how resistant the wider football world is to change, and that in the year of the first semi-professional football league for women in England, the situation remained far from equitable.

Firstly, the Women's World Cup was held in Germany in the summer of 2011. The competition was well received in the media, celebrated for lacking the traits that plague the men's tournaments (theatrics, dissent, conflict between players or fans), its entertainment spectacle and above all else, the quality and competitive nature of the football (Dixon, 2011). There was a great deal of optimism around the England team, with the FAWSL season offering more competitive football and their achievement in the European Championships two years previously. Yet despite all of this, and the efforts made to boost the profile of the women's game, the BBC[8] decided not to show any of the England matches live, instead making them available on their interactive service (not available to all viewers) and website. This was a huge step backwards for the profile of women's football and was widely criticised by those inside and outside of the game (although, perhaps tellingly, not by the FA). England won their group to reach the quarter-finals, which again was not scheduled for live coverage. The BBC instead were showing golf on BBC1 and repeats of comedy show *Porridge* and antiques show *Flog It!* on BBC2 at the time of the match, stressing their policy of not showing sport on both channels at the same time.

Under increasing pressure, including from MPs (Press Association, 2011), the decision not to show the England quarter-final was reversed and the game was screened live (Ashdown & Gibson, 2011). England tried a little too hard to fulfil public expectation of the national football team and lost the match on penalties, but the BBC was applauded for bowing to pressure and screening the match. The whole situation reflects the lack of progress made by the sport, in that it was not deemed necessary for England's matches in a World Cup to be shown on terrestrial television. More concerning was the refusal of the FA to get involved – even justifying the BBC's decision – despite their commitment to enhancing the profile of women's football. The FA commercial director at the time defended the 'scheduling pressures' faced by the BBC.[9]

This overall lack of progress made by women's football was further underlined in the second example from this year. Following their 2006 report into Women's Football, the Department for Culture, Media and Sport (DCMS) Select Committee released the report of its enquiry into

DOI: 10.1057/9781137480323.0007

football governance in England. This report was critical of the lack of progress in some aspects regarding women's football, but the greatest criticism was directed at the lack of diversity at the highest level of the organisation. The FA council, 118 representatives from 'across the game' who met to discuss policy changes, was described as 'lacking diversity' with only two women; equally, the FA National Game board, representing non-professional interests in the game, had no representative from women's football (DCMS, 2011). This was suggested to be 'damaging the FA's ability to take women's football forward' (p. 19). It is not only women who are under-represented in FA decision-making positions, but the lack of admittance of females at this level questions whether the FA are as committed as they claim to be at supporting women's football and making amends for their long and damaging history of female exclusion.

Conclusion

The FAWSL was finally launched in 2011 in what continued to be contradictory and difficult times for women's football. Official participation figures showed a rise in female players at junior and senior levels, yet the game more widely continued to struggle for acceptance. The FAWSL was considered an important step in addressing this struggle by carving out a 'niche' for the sport that would aim to celebrate its differences from men's football – constructing difference as superiority rather than inferiority. The league was celebrated as a success by the FA due to increased exposure and awareness, but this did not mark the beginning of widespread change in the way women's football was perceived. This was however only the start of the journey, and the following year the planned expansion would be announced.

Notes

1   Women's football news, 2 April 2009, http://www.womenssoccerscene.co.uk/womens-football-news-2008-2009/090402-02.htm.
2   http://www.womenssoccerscene.co.uk/womens-football-news-2008-2009/090402-02.htm.
3   http://pitchinvasion.net/blog/2009/08/15/the-womens-premier-league-to-kick-off-under-a-cloud/.

DOI: 10.1057/9781137480323.0007

4 In 1972, US Congress passed Title IX of the Equal Education Amendments Act, which forbade sex discrimination in schools that received federal funding. This gave girls and women access to elite sports programmes and college scholarships. As a result of this legislation, nationwide women's elite school soccer programmes grew exponentially. Colleges 'became the ultimate nurturing ground for maturing athletes' (De varona, 2003: 8–9).

5 For the FA review of the launch, including video footage, see http://www.fawsl.com/news/wsl_launches_at_wembley.html.

6 The Scottish Premier League is the top male professional football division in Scotland.

7 Blackburn Rovers, who could not put a bid together despite playing in the top flight of women's football for the previous four seasons, struggled to keep players for what was effectively a demotion to the second tier below the FAWSL. This resulted in their relegation from the WPL at the end of 2010–2011, only a few weeks after their contemporaries of the previous season were kicking off their FAWSL campaign. Leeds Carnegie, who also did not apply for a 2011 FAWSL place due to an unwillingness from their university 'partners' to commit to the financial requirements, saw a similar exodus of players as well as a breakdown in their relationship with Leeds Metropolitan University and a subsequent re-integration with Leeds United FC (Leighton, 2010c). Nottingham Forest reported that their move out of top-flight football made it more difficult to attract potential sponsors as they were no longer playing in the top league (Leighton, 2011a); their financial problems continued and they again saw their FAWSL application rejected in 2013.

8 The British Broadcasting Corporation (BBC) broadcasts its two main channels, BBC1 and BBC2 on terrestrial television (free to air) and is part-funded by mandatory licence payments by viewers.

9 http://www.u.tv/news/BBC-under-pressure-to-show-womens-World-Cup-quarter-final/7c6a8286-bd48-4ff2-ab90-57874f1da2c6.

DOI: 10.1057/9781137480323.0007

3

The Expansion of the FAWSL

Abstract: *In 2014, the FAWSL was expanded to include a second division, allowing for promotion and relegation between the top two leagues of women's football (but remaining closed off from the rest of the sport in England). This chapter looks at the rollout of the second division of the FAWSL, new for 2014, which has introduced an element of promotion and relegation to this elite competition. It explores the FA's public reasoning behind this expansion, and the minimum requirements specified for licence applications, using their documentation; and examines the effect of the FAWSL's expansion on players, offering greater opportunities for professionalisation and improved contract details and the suggested impact on the England team. The increased obligation for female clubs to build relationships with male football clubs is focussed on in particular detail, as this trend is having (and has historically had) a significant impact on women's teams.*

Dunn, Carrie and Joanna Welford. *Football and the FA Women's Super League: Structure, Governance and Impact.* Basingstoke: Palgrave Macmillan, 2015. DOI: 10.1057/9781137480323.0008.

DOI: 10.1057/9781137480323.0008

Introduction

In 2014, the FAWSL was expanded to include a second division, allowing for promotion and relegation between the top two leagues of women's football (but remaining closed off from the rest of the sport in England). This chapter explores the FA's public reasoning behind this expansion, and the minimum requirements specified for licence applications, using their documentation. It analyses the links between men's and women's football clubs, which in the new structure is an attempt to ensure the sustainability and security of FAWSL teams. It also looks at the effect of the FAWSL's expansion on players, offering greater opportunities for professionalisation and improved contract details, and the suggested improvement this could have on the England team.

The FA's strategy for women's football

The FA's Game Changer Strategy (2012a) set out its five-year plan to encourage the strength and progress of women's football in England. This was presented as a watershed moment for the game, following up on the success of the sport at the London 2012 Olympics, and also marking 20 years since the FA took control of the game.

The strategy described a 'strong women's game' as a cornerstone of the next phase of development, and outlined how this was to be achieved by highlighting five key areas of growth. First, the FA announced the future creation of an elite performance unit under an elite performance director (who had not been appointed at the time of the strategy publication, but has since – former England caretaker manager Brent Hills, working closely with ex-international Marieanne Spacey). Second, they stressed the importance of putting into practice a new commercial strategy, working with supportive commercial partners. Third and fourth, the strategy highlighted the need to grow participation and grow the fanbase, again emphasising the need for media, broadcast and commercial partnerships; but there was a notable absence of discussion of the development of the game from its grassroots.

The WSL 'brochure'

The fifth element of the strategy was the introduction of a second tier of elite women's football in England, the WSL2. This idea was elaborated

DOI: 10.1057/9781137480323.0008

on in the FA's subsequent brochure (2013a), in which they outlined their aims and methods for raising the standards of women's football in England at all levels. They argued for the introduction of a second tier, allowing promotion and relegation between the two, describing it as the launch of a 'summer football pyramid' ('closed and separate' from the rest of the women's football pyramid, which continues to operate on a winter season, similar to men's football). The brochure detailed plans for a 'flexible' schedule, suggesting that there would be plenty of midweek games played in the evening 'to help secure the best spectator attendances possible'.

It also gave an indication of the kind of facilities that WSL clubs would be expected to have, suggesting that they should 'secure facilities with pitches of the highest quality and to forge effective partnerships with facility providers'. There was specific mention made of appropriate usage agreements, pitch improvement and maintenance programmes; the latter was described as particularly important to keep grounds in optimum condition all year round. This may seem an odd requirement when, as we have already indicated, the WSL is a summer league; but as the rest of the domestic and most of the continental leagues continue to operate in winter, WSL clubs will still be required to play in tournaments then, including the FA Women's Cup and the UEFA Champions League. This means that, rather unusually, the players in the FAWSL will often be expected to compete all year round.

Location was also mentioned as an important factor for the FA when considering applications, with potential fanbase a key determining factor. Their explanation – 'grounds with better access and in areas of higher population will be more likely to secure regular, higher attendances' – may seem somewhat superficial to the casual reader; and we will return to this issue around density of population and the likelihood of high attendances and a devoted fanbase later.

The brochure suggested that WSL clubs should act as 'beacons' of best practice for women's football, showing how a club could develop into a financially profitable business, with strong links to the community, and improving the standard of elite women's football in England. However, they took pains to point out that there would be a higher level of expectation on WSL1 clubs than on WSL2 clubs, and that licences for each tier would be likely to be awarded accordingly, explaining: 'FAWSL2 clubs are likely to be a mix of amateur and semi-professional clubs committed to narrowing the gap with FAWSL1 clubs – both on and off the pitch.'

DOI: 10.1057/9781137480323.0008

It also hinted at possible future, further expansion, suggesting that clubs within the winter pyramid could potentially join the WSL set-up. Perhaps significantly, highlighting the experimental and ground-breaking nature of the WSL plans, the brochure also indicates that there may be opportunities for new clubs to join 'should a club ever need to be replaced'. However, it is also suggested that the rigorous application process would guard against any potential failure: 'All new entrants will have to prove themselves via an application process to give the league and clubs the best possible chance of success.'

These undertakings are, obviously, likely to require some investment; and the FA's brochure pledged the possibility of support through the Club Development Fund. Grants from this source would need to be matched by clubs through sponsorship, gate receipts and 'partnerships' with out-side parties, including commercial sponsors. Indeed, the opportunities offered by partnerships are stressed throughout, and there is much men-tion made of the potential offered by partnering with men's clubs, which the FA argues will fast-track the improvement of standards.

The application process

After setting out the principles behind the WSL concept and its expan-sion into two divisions, the FA's brochure invites applications from clubs to become members. Although this may sound like a closed-shop pro-cedure and thus different from the men's leagues, in fact men's clubs are also ostensibly 'members' of their leagues. However, the men's leagues have open promotion and relegation between the Premier League, the Football League and the non-league pyramid, rather than the closed sys-tem the FA specify for the WSL. Although the men's Football League does have 'membership criteria', such as ground specifications, in practice the process is mostly seamless (Stevenage Borough secured promotion from the Conference to the Football League in 1996 but were not permitted entry due to insufficient facilities).

The required application process was described in scant detail, though it was intended to be 'open and transparent'. The brochure was clear that all clubs wishing to be part of either tier had to apply – including those already in the existing WSL structure – but added that an existing WSL licence did not mean an automatic placing in WSL1: 'it will be the strength of their bid that determines if and where they are placed...all

DOI: 10.1057/9781137480323.0008

applications, old and new, will be reviewed as part of the same process.' Applications were open to any new or existing club, provided they
are affiliated to an English County FA. This implied encouragement of
newly established clubs is significant; for entry to the FAWSL, footballing excellence and firm community roots are not necessary. This was
emphasised by the application procedure itself – the submission of a
Club Development Plan, which clearly suggests that hypothetical plans
for the future are more important for this WSL expansion than a proven
track record.

The Club Development Plan required a clear demonstration of how
clubs will meet the minimum requirements in four key areas, necessary
to be addressed in order to achieve an FA licence for either WSL division: financial and business management; commercial sustainability and
marketing; facilities; and players, support staff and youth development.
Thus Club Development Plans had to include at the very least: accounts
and financial forecasts as well as information about the club's intended
sources for match-funding the FA's investment; the club's legal ownership
and management structure details; professional staff details, including
management, marketing, coaching and medical personnel; a business
development and marketing plan, outlining both a future target audience and past spectator attendances; a definition of the club's regional
catchment area, with details of the projected maximum potential spectator base; facility details and ground maintenance plans; and regional and
youth development programme links.

The brochure detailed how the applications would be assessed,
explaining that they would be considered by 'a selection panel comprising independent members and FA representatives with relevant skills
and experience'. However, the FA also emphasised the minimal nature
of the 'minimum requirements', stressing that going beyond these will
increase their chance of success. The successful applicants would be
awarded a four-year club licence, but their progress would be monitored
and subject to annual review.

The FA outlined the intent to assess each application as if the club
was applying for WSL1 entry, unless a club specifically stated that they
only wished to be considered for WSL2. They explained: 'Clubs meeting
FAWSL1 criteria will be considered for a place in the first division. Clubs
that do not meet FAWSL1 criteria but do meet FAWSL2 criteria will be
considered for FAWSL2. Clubs that do not meet the criteria for either
division will not be eligible for a club licence.'

DOI: 10.1057/9781137480323.0008

As is evident from this, there was no specification at this point about how many clubs would be in each division; but the WSL was initially founded with eight teams, which gave an indication about the limited number of places that might be on offer. There was also a veiled warning about local rivals submitting applications: 'Where there are competing applications from the same regional catchment area, the panel will assess the region's capacity to commercially sustain more than one FA WSL club.'

Links to men's football clubs

Linking to men's football clubs is an important feature of the FAWSL – emphasised more in the 2014 application process than the original 2011 one – and deserves considered attention due to the potential impact of this. A briefing document from the FA produced in 2010 prior to the FAWSL launch made it clear that the new league in England would be very different to the organisation of women's football in the USA, in that women's clubs in England would work with men's clubs (The FA, 2010). The obligation to be affiliated to a men's club is unique in Europe; other leagues across the continent do have male–female club links but these are not grown out of necessity (Bayle et al., 2013). This, as explained further later, can significantly alter the dynamics of the relationship. The FAWSL launch document also acknowledged that some people may have concerns about a 'huge imbalance' between the teams operating relatively independently and those being 'bankrolled by men's teams'. The FA addressed this worry by pointing to the high minimum standards expected from clubs and the 'robust application and adjudication process' for licences.

Indeed, their reflection (The FA, 2012c) after the first season of the FAWSL continued to tread a fine line between acknowledging the necessity of some clubs to be supported by men's teams and emphasising the importance of women's football's need to be taken seriously in its own right. They pointed out, correctly, that '[in] terms of league and club finances, commercial investment, popularity, broadcast coverage and awareness' the women's game and the men's game cannot seriously be compared in England at this point, adding that the WSL initiative was intended to present women's football as 'attractive and distinct in its own right', with a brand specifically intended to attract young women and

DOI: 10.1057/9781137480323.0008

families. However, conversely the document also holds up the 'national popularity of and accessibility of male football in England' as something that women's football should also be aiming for.

Encouraging women's clubs to develop partnerships with men's clubs is of great interest, primarily because this has had limited success in England in the past – for some women's clubs and teams it has been very much to their detriment. The infancy and amateur status women's football combined with the well-established and visibly dominant structures of men's football means that most women's clubs become affiliated with male clubs to gain access to the required facilities and resources (Williams, 2003). This is something that has increased significantly at the top level of the game since the FA takeover in 1993. Doncaster Belles, the most successful women's club of the 1980s and early 1990s, began to see their domination challenged by Fulham, Charlton and later Arsenal at this time: teams affiliated with male football clubs. This trend was questioned by the DCMS in their report into women's football in 2006, highlighting that although there were some positive examples of support provided to female clubs by male professional clubs – such as Arsenal – there were equally examples of where this relationship had failed completely (DCMS, 2006).

One high-profile example is how Charlton FC ended the funding to their successful women's section after being relegated from the Premier League in 2007.[1] This was not the first case of an elite men's football club withdrawing funding from their women's section – the previous year, Fulham saw their funding from the men's club withdrawn, funding which had seen them become the first professional women's team in the country. These elite examples are accompanied by many other problems further down the pyramid (Welford, 2008, 2013), with issues currently being faced by Leeds United Ladies the most recent.[2] There is a huge risk associated with partnering with a male football club and becoming reliant on their contribution. Future England captain Casey Stoney played for Charlton at the time their funding was withdrawn, and expressed concern that this could cause 'serious trouble' for the women's game if it were to start happening at other clubs (Leighton, 2007a). Eni Aluko, who also played for Charlton at the time, expressed similar concern at the lack of financial protection provided to women's clubs (Kessel, 2008).

Female clubs seeking to build relationships with professional male football clubs are not unique to England. There are examples of women's football clubs across Europe that are integrated to various extents with male football clubs, and despite important contextual differences,[3] these add weight to the need for these relationships to be monitored and critically examined. The rebranding of the UEFA Women's Cup to the UEFA Women's Champions League in 2009 led to an increase in interest from male professional clubs (Senaux, 2011). Aoki et al. (2010) investigated and profiled various elite European clubs in order to identify best structural practices and 'map the progress to professionalisation' (p. 8). Although a great deal may have changed at individual clubs in the time since this report, it concluded that although integration with male clubs can bring the benefits of resources and exposure, women's teams can simultaneously lose some control over their management strategy. As Welford (2008, 2013) discovered at the grassroots (participatory) level of the sport in England, the degree of integration between male and female clubs at the elite level is essential. Olympique Lyonnaise, currently ranked the top European women's club by UEFA,[4] is considered one of the most successful examples of collaboration between a male and female football club (Bayle et al., 2013). The club has an integrated administrative, sporting and commercial strategy, and has enjoyed on-field success nationally and internationally since joining the male club in 2004 (Senaux, 2011). However, other clubs, where only partial integration is practised – Bayle et al. (2013) give the examples of ADO Den Haag in the Netherlands and FC Zurich in Switzerland – problems can arise due to conflict or crisis between the different sections or financial instability.

The fragility of male–female club associations, even at the top level of the sport, raises some serious questions concerning the integration of women into existing male dominated structures at club level. However, as FA documentation shows, at the elite level of women's football, links are now more essential than ever before; to meet strict FAWSL criteria the support of a male professional football club is of huge benefit, if not 'necessary' in theory. FA General Secretary Alex Horne recently stressed that the involvement of male professional clubs will play a huge part in encouraging more participation in women's and girls' football (The Premier League, 2014), having previously stated that the evolution of a professional league would depend to an extent on the commitment of top clubs where the enthusiasm for women's football is mixed (Gibson, 2012).

DOI: 10.1057/9781137480323.0008

Impact on players domestically

Improving the standard of women's football was one of the aims of the creation of the WSL. The 2010 briefing document suggested that better pitch conditions would contribute to this, and that a summer league would attract more fans, who would not be distracted by their own playing or coaching commitments (within the winter schedule). Establishing a small number of elite clubs would ensure their long-term commercial viability, and these benefits would have a trickle-down effect to the grassroots of women's football as standards improved off and on the pitch, with role models emerging for girls and young women to emulate.

Clubs were also encouraged to think long term about their salaries which, as discussed in the previous chapter, should be paid in full by the club rather than the FA financial contribution. The development plan guidelines (2013a) outlined what clubs needed to bear in mind when considering their playing staff: an indicative player list, including junior internationals; contract details for each of them, including any centrally contracted players; any non-contract players; unnamed players intended to be recruited to the club in the near future; players judged as 'home-grown', who either signed for the club directly from a linked, regional centre of excellence or who have played with the club for at least three years; potential signings from overseas, including EU players; the cumulative anticipated salary costs.

Impact on the England team

This increased professionalism of elite women's football has from the outset also been intended to improve the standard of the England representative team. It is notable that the wish to improve the England team was also one of the reasons given for establishing the then-breakaway men's Premier League in 1992; and it is, of course, equally notable that the men's team has failed to succeed in any international tournament since then.

It is perhaps particularly significant then that the Club Development Plan guidelines (2013a), which inform clubs that to be part of the WSL set-up they should have 'full squad pitch-based sessions at least twice each week', also make specific mention of the necessity to introduce tailored training programmes to meet the elite needs of senior international

DOI: 10.1057/9781137480323.0008

players. It mentions that additional assistance, including workshops and sample programmes, will be available from the FA's International Department to help clubs do this to a high standard.

Conclusion

This chapter has outlined how the WSL has expanded since its inception. The initial success of the eight-team WSL and the FA's long-term plan to improve girls' and women's football in England has led to the introduction of a second tier to the set-up; however, as the next chapter will show, the application process we have outlined has created several problems for clubs, and the decisions made have triggered some anger and confusion from clubs as well as other interested parties and stakeholders.

Notes

1 Charlton Athletic FC adopted three-time FA Premier League champions, Croydon WFC, in 2000; the club won the WFA Cup twice as Croydon and once as Charlton, from seven finals. Charlton reached three consecutive league cup finals up to the season 2005–2006, winning two, and were close to gaining their first ever place in European competition at the time of the financial withdrawal in June 2007.

2 Leeds Ladies have had a particularly turbulent relationship with Leeds United FC throughout the history. Whilst playing at the top level of the game in 2006, all financial support was suddenly ended, and the club denied them access to vital resources such as training facilities, Leeds Ladies became linked to Leeds Metropolitan University and changed their name to Leeds Carnegie (but played in the same Leeds United kit). This relationship then came to an end when they were not in the position to financially support a FAWSL bid, leaving Leeds Ladies again with no support structure. They then returned in sort to Leeds United, receiving funding through the Leeds United Foundation, the community arm of the club. In July 2014, following the appointment of new chairman Massimo Cellino, this support was withdrawn, including any permission to use the name, crest and kit of Leeds United. Donations from fans and others collected to the club ensured that it still survives, although their situation remains precarious.

3 In contrast to the UK, where almost all major sports clubs are dedicated to a single sport, football clubs in many European countries tend to be multi-sport clubs with male and female teams in several sports. For example, FC Bayern

DOI: 10.1057/9781137480323.0008

Munich, although best known for their football team that plays in the German Bundesliga, also have basketball, chess, handball, table tennis and other sports divisions for both men and women. See http://www.fcbayern.de/en/club/club/other-sports/. Spanish club FC Barcelona is also a multi-sports club, with other professional and amateur teams in sports such as basketball, roller hockey, handball, rugby, cycling, athletics, volleyball and baseball (Hamil et al., 2010). Further, both of these clubs as well as many others in Germany are member-owned – fans represent the majority ownership, not companies or single benefactors.

4 http://www.uefa.com/MultimediaFiles/Download/competitions/General/01/96/56/85/1965685_DOWNLOAD.pdf.

DOI: 10.1057/9781137480323.0008

4

The FAWSL2 Controversy: Doncaster Belles and Lincoln Ladies

Abstract: *This chapter looks at the reaction to the decision-making process that left Doncaster Belles outside the FAWSL1 and moved Lincoln Ladies across the Midlands to become Notts County Ladies. These two case studies are important for discussing the impact that decisions that the FA make about the WSL can have on clubs, players, fans, cities and most importantly, perceptions of women's football more widely. It considers the extent of the resistance against the governance of elite women's football in England since the introduction of the two-division structure to the FA Women's Super League.*

Dunn, Carrie and Joanna Welford. *Football and the FA Women's Super League: Structure, Governance and Impact.* Basingstoke: Palgrave Macmillan, 2015. DOI: 10.1057/9781137480323.0009.

Introduction

The previous two chapters have provided the context for the launch of the FAWSL, reflecting on the aims, objectives and format, particularly the expansion to two tiers in 2014. This chapter begins to look beyond this to the impact that the overall structure can have on the game more widely and clubs in particular. To do this we focus on two case studies, Doncaster Belles and Lincoln Ladies.

Doncaster Belles and their demotion

Doncaster Rovers Belles have a long history, extending back to 1969. The club tells the story that the then Belle Vue Belles were originally formed by girls who were selling raffle tickets to the fans at Doncaster Rovers matches. This was, of course, long before the FA took over the running of women's football in England; and despite the tie to Rovers, Belles operate fully independently of the men's side in Doncaster, and always have. However, they do now have a formal partnership with the men's club, adding the 'Rovers' to their name, sharing the Keepmoat community stadium with them and wearing the same kit, but retaining financial and strategic independence.

Belles' long history has been steeped in success. They joined the National League in the 1991–1992 season, and wrapped up a league and cup double without losing a game, demonstrating their on-field dominance, and completed another double in 1993–1994. Gillian Coultard, their captain, also captained England, gaining 119 international caps in her career; Karen Walker, their centre-forward, spent 20 years with the club and scored 40 goals for England. The team's incredible record-breaking feats even drew mainstream media attention, with a BBC TV documentary 'The Belles' screened in January 1995, and Pete Davies' book *I Lost My Heart to the Belles* (2006) inspiring the successful television series *Playing the Field*. They were one of the founder members of the FAWSL in 2011.

In April 2013, however, it was announced that following the decision to restructure elite women's football into two divisions, and an application process which involved written submissions (from all existing and potential new clubs) plus an interview panel, Belles would be competing in FAWSL2 instead of FAWSL1: relegation in all but name. The FA

DOI: 10.1057/9781137480323.0009

explained their decision in a statement dated 29 June 2013,[1] outlining three major objections: the Belles' use of the Keepmoat as third priority; the Belles' failure to produce a satisfactory commercial and marketing plan and Belles' intent for 11% of turnover to go on paying players, which the FA did not think was sufficient (the FA cap for WSL clubs is currently 40%).

Belles appealed the decision immediately, objecting vociferously to the composition of the FA Selection panel, which made the decision (it comprised three people from the FA, one independent). The FA argued in response (FA, 2013c) that their earlier statement that the panel would comprise 'independent members and FA representatives with relevant skills and experience' was in a brochure and thus not contractually binding.

The FA panel review report was also strongly and perhaps unusually critical of Belles' vice-chairman Alan Smart and his role in the process. They also criticised the club's failure to seek proper legal advice, and their response suggested that Belles' objections should have been raised prior to the interview process instead of after.[2]

Fan reaction

Unsurprisingly, there was a vociferous response to what was perceived as a demotion for the Belles; and in this next section we shall address some of the reactions and the channels through which they were voiced.

▸ Fan-run websites

Perhaps the most significant and long-lasting response was from Popular Stand, a Doncaster Rovers fan site, who, obviously, had a particularly strong interest in the decision. They objected to the decision from the outset, through the appeals process, and continued to write about the issue, using social media to engage with other people interested in it. Their first article, published in May 2013, noted their feeling that the Belles had been '[s]hafted and scratched out' and suggested that the FA did not care about the Belles' history or work establishing the women's game in England.[3] Similarly, following the appeal, Popular Stand's Glen Wilson wrote an article which was highly critical of the FA and their 'ruthlessness', and complimentary of the Belles' football heritage as well as their position in the community.[4]

DOI: 10.1057/9781137480323.0009

The groundswell of public outrage and the vast amount of site traffic they were attracting led them to set up an online petition, entitled 'Against the FA's Unfair "Relegation" of the Doncaster Belles', but they also urged readers to support Belles in person: 'They are the town's top-ranked football team, they are committed to this community, and they deserve your support.' There was a physical protest planned for the 2013 FA Women's Cup Final, to be held at the Belles' Keepmoat Stadium. However, stewards confiscated flyers, petitions and banners, muting the planned demonstration (WSC, 2013b).

Objections were not limited simply to Doncaster Rovers supporters. The FA's decision was also criticised by other fan forums, such as Twohundredpercent, a website covering the business and culture of football, who described the FA's treatment of Belles as a 'betrayal' (2013).

▸ FSF reaction

The Football Supporters' Federation also addressed the issue with an online article from one of its national council members, Tim Hillyer, published on 14 June 2013, prior to the appeal. It was based on a meeting with Kelly Simmons, head of the women's national game for the FA, and one of the panel members who had made the initial decision to put Belles into FAWSL2. Hillyer's article was careful to address only the facts as presented at this point, going through the detail of the licensing procedure. However, perhaps some evidence of partiality emerged in the closing paragraph: 'From what I learned from Kelly Simmons, and reading much of the documentation, the best hope for the Belles lies in putting together and delivering the very best appeal. Good luck to them.'[5]

▸ Media reaction

A broad range of mainstream media covered the initial decision and the appeal process. Local news stories reported outraged comments from the likes of Vic Akers, the former Arsenal Ladies manager, who was quoted by the Thorne and District Gazette as describing the decision as 'morally scandalous'.[6] However, there was also national media interest; perhaps because Belles have been part of the national sporting landscape for so long with that historic level of media coverage in the 1990s, but perhaps also because the fan protest planned for the FA Women's Cup Final, to be held at the Keepmoat, was potentially an excellent story.

DOI: 10.1057/9781137480323.0009

Martin Cloake for the *New Statesman* (2013) described the initial decision as 'scandalous', sweeping aside 'one of the basic principles of sporting success, sentenced a club to a season of playing matches in a campaign it has already lost', and making an effort to prevent any kind of protest.[7] Laura Williamson of the *Daily Mail* (2013), again writing before the appeal, referred to the decision as 'a gross betrayal of everything sport should be about', and something that would not happen in men's football. She predicted the appeal's outcome with the scathing conclusion: 'Oh, and that "independent panel"? They are chosen by the FA and will convene at Wembley. Good luck to the Belles – they'll need it.'[8]

Reflections on public reactions

As the previous section has made very clear, the public reaction has been strongly in favour of the Belles and against authorities. This response has been evident from fans, the media, and other people involved in football, but it has had no effect. The FA's decision was binding, and Doncaster Belles have taken their places in FAWSL2. *The Telegraph* described Belles' appeal against the FA as a battle for the 'soul of football',[9] but it is a battle which the FA won outright, without having to fight too hard at all.

The next section looks at our second case study: Lincoln Ladies' move across the Midlands to become Notts County Ladies.

Lincoln Ladies rebrand as Notts County for 2014

Lincoln has had a ladies' team since 1995 when they began playing regional football. They quickly progressed through the leagues to the FA WPL Northern division (second tier), from where they successfully applied for a FAWSL place in 2009. They were one of the founder eight teams in the FAWSL, although their involvement in the top league did mean that they effectively 'jumped' above teams in the WPL to play at this level.

Throughout their history, Lincoln Ladies had a mixed relationship with the male club Lincoln City FC. They first became associated in the mid-1990s, and wore the kit and had the crest of the male club. In 2003, they became the first women's club to play a full season at a professional Football League stadium when they played their home games at Sincil

DOI: 10.1057/9781137480323.0009

Bank, home of Lincoln City. For the following seasons, they played on various male team pitches until their return to Sincil Bank for the FAWSL season in 2011, although they divided their time between there and non-league ground Ashby Avenue. The year 2013 saw another return to Sincil Bank (by which time Lincoln FC were no longer in the Football League) for what was to be the final season of top-flight ladies' football in Lincoln.

Ray Trew, former director and chairman of Lincoln City FC (men's team), is widely credited for the success of Lincoln to this point, giving considerable financial backing and sponsorship through his company (which led to them being called OOH Lincoln before the FAWSL proposal). Trew joined Lincoln Ladies' committee in 2006, three years after joining the men's club, although he left his role at Lincoln City the same year after a boardroom dispute. He then saw a takeover bid of the men's club rejected. In 2010, he purchased Notts County FC, the oldest football team in the world still playing professionally, located 40 miles from Lincoln in Nottingham. He did however continue to financially support Lincoln Ladies and is credited as the driving force behind their FAWSL bid.[10]

After two full seasons in the FAWSL, in which they finished fourth and fifth respectively, the application process opened for the 2014 licence. In April 2013, after one week of the third FAWSL season, it was announced that Lincoln had successfully applied for a place in the FAWSL 2014 as Notts County (This is Lincolnshire, 2013). The announcement was final, and came as a shock to a great deal of fans (although some responses[11] suggest that this was an inevitable outcome of Trew moving to Notts County). An FA embargo prevented any explanation of the decision, frustrating Lincoln fans, until three months later when an article named 'Notts County Ladies Vision' appeared on the Notts County FA website.[12] This states that the rebranding was necessary to meet the required application criteria, with 'key areas that we could only fulfill [sic] by relocating' and pointing to the 'shared Chairman Ray Trew' who was 'welcoming of the idea to share the resources of both of his clubs for their mutual gain'. The statement suggests that having a partnership with a male football club is becoming increasingly important for FAWSL clubs (as discussed in the previous chapter). Indeed the BT Sport (who acquired the FAWSL rights from 2014) profile of Notts County LFC states that 'the team decided to move to Nottingham because they were required to have a link to a male team for the new two-tier WSL'.[13] As

DOI: 10.1057/9781137480323.0009

with Doncaster Belles, Lincoln played the 2013 season out following the announcement of the decision. After a perhaps unsurprisingly poor start to the season, Lincoln finished sixth in their third and final year in the FAWSL.

Notwithstanding local protestations, the decision remained final and the last 'Lincoln Ladies' match was the 2013 Continental Cup Final where they lost to Arsenal. Notts County started their first FAWSL season in April 2014, with a squad made up of a mixture of Lincoln Ladies players and new signings, including England internationals Ellen White and Carly Telford. Some big Lincoln names departed before the start of the 2014 season, notably captain Casey Stoney who joined Arsenal. Notts County Ladies played their first season at Meadow Lane, the home stadium of the male club.

Fan reaction

Similar to the Belles case, fan reaction to the Lincoln Ladies move to Notts County has been considerable, and highly critical of the decision (see, for example, BBC Sport, 2013). However, the situation differs greatly in that it is the club (or the owner) that the fans are angry with, not the governing body – despite it fundamentally being the FA licensing system, application requirements and their acceptance of relocation and rebranding that has created the situation. Anger at the club has created a situation where fans feel able to 'vote with their feet' – stop supporting the club – whereas the Doncaster Belles reaction has arguably solidified the relationship with the club and fan base. In the Belles case, fans were also encouraged to 'vote with their feet', but in this case in the opposite respect – attending games to demonstrate how well supported they were.

Lincoln fans took to the Internet to vent their anger utilising social media, forums and club websites to highlight their displeasure and the ending of their support for the club.[14] Protests were however confined predominantly to the local area – the issue did not gain the extent of national coverage that the Doncaster Belles case did, which limited the reach of the story. With no formal appeal channel to vent their frustration – Lincoln fans had nobody to appeal to, as the move was sanctioned and supported by all parties involved – expressing their disappointment over Internet-based channels of communication was all that was

DOI: 10.1057/9781137480323.0009

available to them. Our reflection on the content of their comments are discussed below alongside the media content, as these often overlapped and together, give a comprehensive overview of the reaction to the decision to rebrand.

Media reaction

The issue received good coverage in the local press, with a number of articles discussing the impact of the move to Notts County on the local area. A couple of specialist women's football blogs covered the issue, but the 'decision is final' situation perhaps contributed to the limited interest in the story, particularly when compared to the case of Doncaster Belles and their appeal against the FA. Players used the media interest to 'apologise' to fans (see, for example, Magowan, 2013), with nothing more than a subtle undertone of dissatisfaction to the decision on their part. They had a full season to play as Lincoln Ladies, so any frustrations that they might have had could not be expressed.

Unsurprisingly, the local Lincolnshire press were highly critical of the move. Former managers, players and fans were quoted to support the expressed dissatisfaction at the decision, and a reflective piece written two weeks after the decision was announced proclaimed in its headline that 'Supporters will not follow the club to Nottingham' (Lincolnshire Echo, May 2013). The article summed up the local feeling as one of 'sadness', referring to 'loyal fans that have been left behind' and asking whether the team will get as much support (from fans as well as the media) in a city with a more saturated sporting market. (Early spectator figures on the 2014 season[15] actually place Notts County as the club with the highest average attendance at just under 1000, so this concern at least appears unfounded.)

National broadsheet *The Guardian* ran a piece on the rebrand shortly after the decision was announced (Riach, 2013), and BBC Sport followed suit in response to the long-awaited statement from Notts County explaining the decision behind the move. Both articles referred to fan discontent and the recent changes in the women's game that reflect greater significance to the business side of the game and the importance of male club links, although *The Guardian* reflected the greater criticism of the decision. It was described as sparking a 'franchise fury', with reference to the case of MK Dons in English men's football, a club formed

DOI: 10.1057/9781137480323.0009

when the former Wimbledon FC needed to find a new home.[16] Lincoln Ladies' chief executive was quoted as saying that the fan reaction reflects 'initial annoyance', playing down the move as 'only 30 miles away' (Riach, 2013).

Reflections on the reaction to the move

In reflecting on the Internet-based fan reaction to the move to Nottingham, there is very clear and obvious criticism of the decision, but as highlighted earlier, this is directed overwhelmingly at the club owner and clubs involved rather than the FA. The fan and media reactions highlight the perceived extent of the impact of the move, with a number of implications suggested for the club, the city, women's football (and even men's football) and football supporters more widely.

▸ The Lincoln fan base

The vast majority of fans who commented online stated that they would no longer be supporting Lincoln after they moved to Notts County, with a good proportion professing to be severing their ties straight after the announcement (and therefore not supporting Lincoln for the 2013 season). Whilst in some cases this may have been an emotive knee-jerk reaction to the announcement – and reflecting the only option for protest available to them in 'voting with their feet' – it is understandable that Lincoln-based supporters would have to seriously consider whether they can continue to attend matches that would involve an 80-mile round trip.

The most vociferous fans on the Lincoln City FC (men's club) forums gave strong reasons for their difficulty in supporting Notts County. For those who supported Lincoln Ladies because of their support for Lincoln City (men), supporting Notts County would involve cheering on one of their rivals. For the Lincoln Ladies fan base, issues revolved more around the travel required to continue supporting the club. Women's football is still young, with many of the top clubs enjoying only a recent history. They therefore often do not have established fan bases that would stick by them regardless (perhaps with the notable exception of Doncaster Belles). In comparison, male football club support is often tied to family links, with generations supporting the same club, creating bonds that are very hard to break. This is a crucial difference when judging the likelihood of fans continuing to support a club in this situation.

DOI: 10.1057/9781137480323.0009

Fans were also angry at the lack of consultation and consideration given to them. Even if this should not have come as a complete surprise, fans were given no official advance warning of the move which contributed to their reaction, and even after the decision was announced, this continued. The Lincoln Ladies Facebook page was used by fans to ask questions about the impact of the move on them, but any replies were noncommittal and usually stated that no further information could be released at this time. A blog by a Lincoln Ladies supporter on the women's football website SheKicks expresses this feeling succinctly:

> It really feels like we have just been tossed by the wayside. ... The local paper can't find anything out and the website basically says 'wait and see'. I just feel so disgusted by the whole thing. I have so many questions but the main one being why?[17]

▶ Lincoln as a city

Local media focused on the loss of the club to the city. Having an elite football club with national team players was seen as a source of pride to local people and something to celebrate, with one article stating that the county 'had a sports team it could be proud of'.[18] Having the name of the city associated with the elite level of any sport was of benefit to Lincoln. Again, fans who supported Lincoln Ladies as their 'local' team might find it difficult to effectively change their allegiance to a Nottingham team, in the knowledge that any money they give through tickets and merchandise will not be benefiting their home city. Nottingham already have several high-profile sports teams including two professional men's football clubs, a women's team that has played top flight football, rugby league and rugby union teams, an ice hockey team and a county cricket club, so an FAWSL team would have more competition for supporters and might not have the same impact on the city as it did for Lincoln.

Comments from Lincoln Ladies fans also expressed concern on the impact the move might have on the future of talented girls in the area. BBC Lincolnshire ran a video feature[19] on the move and the impact of this on the local area, and a major aspect of the report was the uncertainty over the future of the Centre of Excellence that provides a pathway for talented girls in the local area to progress to elite football. With their exit club now playing in a different city and no local role models on hand to look up to, there was understandable concern about this aspect of the club.

DOI: 10.1057/9781137480323.0009

▶ Existing Nottingham football clubs

As the move was announced on the Notts County FC (men's) club website, this gave the opportunity for fans of the male clubs to comment. Although there was some support for the move – acknowledging the benefit to the club that have a FAWSL team might bring – there was some concern over having another team playing on the Meadow Lane pitch (it is also used by Nottingham rugby union club).

Nottingham local press also had their criticisms of the move, highlighting the impact that it would have on the two existing ladies' teams in the city. Notts County Ladies actually already existed, having played in the East Midlands regional league under the Notts County banner since 2011. The greater criticism, however, was for the impact that the move would have on Nottingham Forest Ladies FC, a club with a history of women's football since the 1970s but that has struggled financially in recent times and seen two FAWSL applications rejected. BBC Nottingham reported that 'Lincoln Ladies' move to Nottingham will "kill Forest Ladies"',[20] criticising the perceived lack of transparency in the bidding process as Nottingham Forest claimed they were unaware that Notts County were applying and that having two clubs from the same city went against them. Failing to secure a place in the FAWSL for a second time was seen as 'limiting' their development to its current state, unable to progress beyond the third tier of women's football without ever having being relegated from the top flight. With competition for supporters in the city now increased with a FAWSL club playing close by, there was a real concern over the future of the club.

▶ Women's football more widely

Fans from Lincoln (men's) team suggested that the move might put fans off women's football generally, seeing it as a 'joke' that a club can be moved in this way and that a city who wants a top-flight club can acquire an existing one rather than having to start at the bottom. Reflecting the desire to protect the traditional pyramid league system, one Lincoln City forum user asked 'why couldn't Notts County form a new club?' and another commented that the rebrand had left them 'totally ambivalent' to women's football.[21]

Reports and comments highlighted a very real fear with women's football, that even in its early stages of (semi-)professionalism it is suffering from the more negative aspects of men's football. The case of MK Dons and their vilification by fans up and down the country for being the 'first franchise club' in football (see, for example, Joyce, 2006) was criticised by many for going against what football is 'supposed to be about': league position based on success and achievement, and clubs rooted in their communities. Modern football is increasingly criticised for the loss of the latter, yet despite the money injection at the top, the former is on the whole retained – with the exception of MK Dons. That arguably the most-feared change in European football, clubs receiving league positions without earning them through merit, is seemingly an unchallengeable feature of women's football is something that will be difficult to reconcile for the football fan.

Allowing clubs to effectively be a franchise to be moved around the country is a major aspect of the FAWSL that 'others' it from male footballing structures. In gauging the response to this issue, there is perhaps the concern that women's football can be more easily dismissed as it is not 'real' football – real football has promotion and relegation, and clubs have to start at the bottom – an issue that the game has faced throughout its development. This is all the more powerful when considered in combination with the Doncaster Belles demotion and Manchester City entering the top FAWSL league as a new team.

Reflections on public reactions

In contrast to the case of Doncaster Belles, the fan reaction to the rebranding of Lincoln Ladies created a significant dislocation between the club and its fan base. Although the move was explained as a direct result of the FAWSL application criteria, the majority of fan discontent was directed at the club, and in particular the owner, despite the fact that he had invested significantly in Lincoln Ladies to get them into the FAWSL. Club identity is important to fans, particularly those with historical ties to a club, and the idea of 'changing' your allegiance to a different club falls outside of fan understandings. For Lincoln Ladies fans, this seems to be the case even though their history is relatively recent.

With respect to maintaining their support, the difficult issue for fans is whether Notts County are understood as a 'new' club or that Lincoln Ladies have moved to a new home. This is a very grey area, and looking at the rebrand as a whole makes things no clearer. In essence, the FAWSL application as Notts County was on behalf of a new club, as this was not

DOI: 10.1057/9781137480323.0009

based on the existing Notts County Ladies at the time. Yet fans were told that Lincoln is simply moving its base to Nottingham, suggesting that the club continues just under a new name. The official statement from Notts County came from this perspective, asking that fans continue 'following the club in our new home' (see Note 2). But the identifying features of a football club – the name, the ground, the kit – all changing make it difficult for any identity to move. Who do past achievements belong to? Does Notts County Ladies have a history, or did its history begin in 2014? These questions run deep to the heart of footballing identities, and have created a difficult situation for Lincoln fans. The discontent suggests that the club formerly known as Lincoln Ladies ended in 2013, despite initial efforts from Notts County to counter this. The history of Lincoln Ladies is now difficult to find – searching 'Lincoln Ladies' on the Internet results in Notts County pages. The FAWSL previous season section on their website have Lincoln listed but the match report links to the Notts County Ladies site. If Notts County are indeed a new club – as their Twitter representative claimed in a blunt reply to criticism earlier this season[22] – then it is unfair that the history of Lincoln Ladies appears to have been wiped from the football history books.

Conclusion

Having explored these two case studies, there are some striking similarities that are worth emphasising. We would like to put forward a number of suggestions as to why this might be. First, perhaps the size and type of cities Doncaster and Lincoln are important in this situation. Having a successful women's football team could be argued to be particularly important to them – neither has a particularly strong men's team or success in other sports, making success in the elite FAWSL a matter of civic pride.

Despite the relative lack of interest from mainstream media (with some notable exceptions, as discussed earlier in this chapter), the fan media reaction to the situations of Doncaster Belles and Lincoln has been extensive, vociferous and continuing; one of the benefits of access to the Internet and social media has meant that fans can set their own news agenda to an extent. However, this response and activism has still been relatively limited (as is pretty much all fan activism) – for example, petitions against the FA's decisions have been circulated with

DOI: 10.1057/9781137480323.0009

comparatively small sign-ups (at the time of writing, Popular Stand's online petition had still not reached 10,000 signatures, over a year after its establishment).

The question is why the broad and vocal objections have not translated into much direct action. One potential reason could be because the FA's appeals process has made it clear that all decisions were at their discretion, regardless of disgruntlement, and therefore people believe there is no possibility of changing the FA's mind.

Another could be because fan activism is and has been viewed as pointless and ineffective. For example, although supporters' trusts have been established in England for well over a decade, often in protest against football clubs' mismanagement, there are still relatively few Premier League and Football League clubs with any kind of supporter representation on the board. In both cases described in this chapter, supporters have done what they can: voted with their feet, in maintaining their support for Doncaster Belles and stopping their support for Lincoln Ladies.

Finally, it could be a much more simple reason: mass, broad interest in and engagement with women's football in England is still relatively new. Belles' history stretches back to 1969, but many men's clubs were founded in the mid-nineteenth century. Women's football was popular in England at the start of the twentieth century, as our earlier chapters have shown, but the ban on women playing has had a systemic, structural effect. Since the FA's choice to finally take over the running of the women's game, the fortunes of the England team have warranted some interest. Their progress to the 2009 European Championships final garnered some interest, as did their good performance in the 2011 World Cup. By the time a combined Team GB competed in the 2012 Olympics, the high-profile likes of Steph Houghton, then of Arsenal Ladies, were deemed newsworthy enough to be pictured on the front of daily newspapers. Despite England's failure at the 2013 European Championships, their games during that tournament and recent World Cup qualifiers, mostly on BBC3, have still got excellent viewing figures.

However, this is not reflected in the domestic game. Club sides still have little coverage, with selected WSL games on digital TV and the FA Cup final on BBC. We suggest, then, that fans of women's football are possibly fans of men's football first, so the women's game comes lower on their list of priorities for action; and for those dedicated enough to want to take action, because there are so few of them, they have little real knowledge of how best to mobilise.

DOI: 10.1057/9781137480323.0009

Notes

1 http://www.thefa.com/News/governance/2013/jun/doncaster-belles-appeal-statement.aspx.

2 The adjudication is available online at http://www.thefa.com/News/governance/2013/jun/~/media/258E9250FB6C497B8DCD46E7E482B83D.ashx.

3 http://popularstand.wordpress.com/2013/05/13/the-belles-toll-on-the-fas-relegation-of-the-doncaster-belles/.

4 http://popularstand.wordpress.com/2013/06/29/silenced-belles-on-the-fas-rejection-of-the-doncaster-belles-appeal/.

5 http://www.fsf.org.uk/blog/view/the-appeal-of-doncaster-belles.

6 http://www.thornegazette.co.uk/sport/local-sport/doncaster-belles-arsenal-s-akers-backs-the-belles-1-5718732.

7 http://www.newstatesman.com/business/2013/07/doncaster-belles-case-showed-us-how-little-fa-understands-what-makes-football-great.

8 http://www.dailymail.co.uk/sport/article-2346937/Doncaster-Belles-betrayed-FA--Laura-Williamson.html.

9 http://www.telegraph.co.uk/sport/football/10142261/Doncaster-Belles-battle-to-save-soul-of-womens-football.html.

10 http://www.thisislincolnshire.co.uk/Lincoln-Ladies-Ex-boss-Rod-Wilson-sad-decision/story-18847342-detail/story.html#axzz2eP2ax990.

11 http://www.lincoln.vitalfootball.co.uk/forum/forums/thread-view.asp?tid=31893&start=17.

12 http://www.nottscountyfc.co.uk/news/article/notts-county-ladies-vision-928926.aspx 18 July 2013.

13 http://sport.bt.com/sportfootball/football/wsl-club-profile-notts-county-ladies-S11363890629413.

14 See, for example, the BBC (2013); http://www.lincoln.vitalfootball.co.uk/forum/forums/thread-view.asp?tid=31893&start=17; http://www.thisislincolnshire.co.uk/Lincoln-Ladies-Notts-County-Ladies-2014/story-18814461-detail/story.html#axzz2eP2ax990.

15 http://www.football-lineups.com/tourn/FA_WSL_2014/stats/home_avg_atte/.

16 When professional male football club Wimbledon continued to struggle to find a suitable home ground, a move to Milton Keynes – a purpose-built town 80 miles from Wimbledon with no league club – was proposed. The FA allowed the move despite vociferous support from the entire football community, not just Wimbledon fans. Wimbledon were rebranded as MK Dons and many fans cannot accept that a club could simply be 'moved' from its community, losing its identity (Joyce, 2006).

17 http://www.shekicks.net/flog/blogs/post/753.

DOI: 10.1057/9781137480323.0009

18   http://www.thisislincolnshire.co.uk/Lincoln-Ladies-Supporters-follow-club-Nottingham/story-18867225-detail/story.html#axzz2eP2ax99o.

19   http://www.bbc.co.uk/news/uk-england-lincolnshire-22365844.

20   http://www.bbc.co.uk/news/uk-england-22352456.

21   http://www.lincoln.vitalfootball.co.uk/forum/forums/thread-view.asp?tid=32224&posts=24.

22   See the twitter conversation at https://twitter.com/Official_NCLFC/status/408980775703302144, which includes a blunt response to the claim from one user that Notts County are in fact still Lincoln Ladies: 'We are Notts County Ladies. The Lincoln Ladies franchise has expired!'

DOI: 10.1057/9781137480323.0009

5
The Media Coverage of the FAWSL: A Girl Thing?

Abstract: *Reports and features on women's sport make up just 5% of media coverage; and studies have regularly come to the same conclusion: the media shows far fewer women than men in a sporting context, and though women's participation in sport has grown, this has not been reflected in an equal expansion of media coverage. This chapter explores how FAWSL players view the media coverage they receive, and shows that players themselves take responsibility for raising their profile, often via social media, and they report that they are very aware of the importance of promoting a positive image not just to secure their own media profiles and to attract more fans to the sport but a desire to inspire young women.*

Dunn, Carrie and Joanna Welford. *Football and the FA Women's Super League: Structure, Governance and Impact.* Basingstoke: Palgrave Macmillan, 2015. DOI: 10.1057/9781137480323.0010.

~~duction~~

Reports and features on women's sport make up just 5% of media coverage (WSFF, 2011). Martin and McDonald (2012) point out that studies have regularly come to the same conclusion: the media shows far fewer women than men in a sporting context, and though women's participation in sport has grown, this has not been reflected in an equal expansion of media coverage.

This chapter focuses primarily on the media coverage of major international women's football tournaments, which should theoretically have the broadest appeal to consumers. It explores how players (all international as well as WSL players) view the media coverage they receive. They discuss the media coverage they have experienced throughout their careers, and report recent improvements, such as media training to help them deal with journalists.

However, they also note that the type of media coverage they receive is important, criticising the continuing emphasis on presenting them as sexualised or 'feminine', as well as heterosexual, and reporting their own experiences of photo shoots and interviews. The chapter demonstrates a difficult negotiation that elite female athletes have to make, combining their personal views with their public-facing roles as spokespeople and public figures.

Women's sport in the media

The FAWSL is not the only example of women's sport that receives a minimal amount of media coverage. This neglect of women's elite sport is endemic and systemic: just 2% of articles and 1% of images in the sports pages of British national newspapers are devoted to female athletes and women's sport (WSFF, 2008). This may be partially attributed to the fact that sport has traditionally been deemed a male and masculine domain; indeed, Semyonov (1981) enthuses about the 'phenomenon' of only one-third of Olympic competitors in 1970 being female, simply because women had initially been banned from the Games altogether. Martin and McDonald (2012) point out that studies have regularly come to the same conclusion: the media shows far fewer women than men in a sporting context, and though women's participation in sport has grown, this has not been reflected in an equal expansion of media coverage.

DOI: 10.1057/9781137480323.0010

Even in the USA, where Title IX has ensured equal funding for women's sports in schools and colleges, the media continues to concentrate attention on men's sports (cf. Kearney, 2011); and coverage of women's sports is in fact declining, with the focus of what little coverage there is being on athletes' conventional heterosexual attractiveness, serving to trivialise their sporting accomplishments (Martin and McDonald, 2012).

Murray and Howat (2009) observe that women may be uncomfortable playing sport because of the 'dissonance' between the 'traditional feminine role' and the 'athletic role ... embedded in traditions of masculinity, competition and aggression'. It is possible that sports editors feel the same way about seeing images and printing text about women playing sport, hence the low level of coverage.

Historical media coverage of women's football

The historical and continuing problem that the English (and more widely British) media has had with covering women's sport is well known and frequently stated. The difficulty they have with covering women competing in a sport they consider typically 'male' – such as football – has received a little less attention.

Even when coverage aims to be positive, the difficulty commentators have with reconciling the 'masculine' sport with 'feminine' participants is evident. This is demonstrated very clearly in an article by professional male footballer David James, then Portsmouth and England goalkeeper, during the Women's World Cup group stage (*The Observer*, 16/09/2007). The clashing of discourses is here particularly evident in the attempts by James to understand the elite level of women's football, despite persistently asserting his support for the game. Although reflecting only the viewpoint of a single male professional footballer and commentator, this article is important in highlighting both the women's game's perceived need of, and complexity resulting from, attempts to gain male support. Moreover, the difficulty in separating women's football from on the one hand, men's football, and on the other, the prevailing notion that women must at all times retain their femininity, is evident throughout. After describing how he and the England squad had been impressed with the quality of the women's games, including 'some John Terry-esque[1] clearances and tackles going in from the England back line', the piece concludes with some apparent praise of Kelly Smith,[2] whom he describes

DOI: 10.1057/9781137480323.0010

as 'a phenomenal player', adding: 'With her positioning on the ball, she wouldn't look out of place in a men's side. One of the lads put it deftly when he said: "She's a manly player – without looking at all manly", which made me chuckle.'

This article highlights both the challenge women pose to the male dominance of football, and the limitations of this challenge due to the dominance of masculine understandings. Equating being a 'phenomenal player' with (usually) being 'manly' limits the subjectivities available to women in football; to be accepted is dependent on being able to 'play like a man' but not 'look like a man'. The norm in football is also reproduced as a male norm that women should aspire to whilst remaining firmly within the boundaries of femininity. Although this book cannot of course produce an in-depth-and-breadth analysis of all media coverage of women's football, this chapter will highlight some of the gendered discourses that are frequently presented in the sports media, and it recognises that these are important manifestations of the issues with which it is concerned. What these media texts highlight are the complexities of women's increased involvement in a sporting arena that has traditionally and constantly excluded them. Despite providing a positive report of male interest in football, the liberal discourse of equal opportunities that is increasingly interpreted as the 'successful' movement of women into an arena they have traditionally been excluded from, masks much deeper complexities concerning the struggle women face in being accepted in their own right outside of the dominant (male) frame of reference.

Media coverage of women's sport is not just important in terms of parity for current achievements, but it also plays a part in establishing positive female role models for children. This aspect about role models is something that is currently under investigation by one of the authors, but suffice to say that the issue of role models for young women has been the subject of popular and academic discussion in recent years, perhaps in popular media most obviously through the 2012 GirlGuiding survey which highlighted that young women simply weren't aware of elite women's sport. Whether or not sporting role models have an impact on encouraging sporting participation, however, is something else which is interrogated by a number of studies without a consensus as yet. As this chapter demonstrates, female footballers themselves speak about their own lack of female sporting role models as children, and now perceive themselves as being able to fill that gap for the next generation.

DOI: 10.1057/9781137480323.0010

We move on to reflect on the London 2012 Olympic Games and the media coverage of women's football at this most high profile of events. It came after the launch of the FAWSL, and seven years after the previous major women's football tournament to be hosted in the British Isles – the 2005 European Championships.

London 2012

The London 2012 Olympic Games provided an opportunity for the British media to showcase the best of women's sport; indeed, the achievements of Team GB women led to newspapers hailing Jessica Ennis as 'a humble heroine who can use [her] heptathlon gold medal... to inspire [a] generation' (*Telegraph*, 2012) and 'the inspirational role model so desperately needed by Britain's young women today... a one woman, seven-discipline, six-pack antidote to the fake, feckless flakes who have cluttered up our popular culture for too long' (*Mirror*, 2012).

Team GB women's football team, although they did not win a medal, impressed the sports reporters too; veteran football writer Henry Winter praised their win against Brazil and described them as 'great role models' not just for their on-pitch performance, but also their conduct off the field (*Telegraph*, 2012).

The FA and the FAWSL immediately picked up on the positive impression that the footballers had made on the media and viewers, using the discourse of the role model in their promotional material for the second half of the FAWSL which resumed in September after the close of the Olympics. In a press release, head of the FA national game Kelly Simmons was quoted as saying: 'We want to encourage everyone to be inspired by the Olympics and keep supporting women's football and the wonderful role models that play the game.'

The players too have employed this same discourse; Team GB and then England captain Casey Stoney has used the vocabulary to urge the media to continue covering women's sports outside of the Olympics (*Metro*, 2013); and the significance of continued media coverage has also been highlighted by Team GB and England's Jill Scott and Ellen White (*Stylist*, 2012).

There have been some significant efforts to increase coverage across various media outlets, but these have been revealed to be inconsistent. The front pages given over to Team GB's women's football squad after

DOI: 10.1057/9781137480323.0010

they defeated Brazil were unique to the London Olympics (as indeed was the Team GB football initiative), indicating that this coverage was more to do with a patriotic acknowledgement of their success for Great Britain in the world's biggest and most high-profile sporting event. The England team's subsequent failure (and the other home nations failing to qualify) at the 2013 European Championships meant that the interest in women's international football was not capitalised on. Even during the 2015 World Cup qualifiers, with Wales and England in the same group, there was little to no newspaper coverage of any matches.

The BBC's coverage of international football, similarly, has been inconsistent; the outcry over their initial failure to schedule coverage of England's World Cup 2011 and Euro 2013 campaigns is discussed elsewhere in this book. They televised only a selection of England's matches during the qualifiers, meaning there was no way for fans to follow the games live. Obviously there are issues around TV rights that may have prevented these broadcasts (or even live-streaming online); but the impression given to the casual observer or the fan is that the national broadcaster is only intermittently interested in women's international football. \

These developments set the background to the original research quoted in the rest of this chapter; the study began by talking to footballers, all of whom were currently playing at domestic and international levels, with some taking part in the 2012 Olympics. All have been pseudonymised, and any detail that could identify them specifically has been removed.

Media coverage of women's football in the Olympics

Liz was surprised by the amount of interest in women's football during the Olympics.

> Yeah, I don't think any of us really expected it to be quite in the media as it was, really. I think it really helped us in terms of we literally kicked off the Olympics, we were the first kind of sport to play at the Olympics, and that kind of gave us a platform to be put in the papers, all across the back pages, Steph [Houghton] was everywhere, so it was good for us to get that kind of exposure right before the Olympics actually properly started, so that was a massive platform for us, and it just kind of grew and grew as the Olympics moved on really, and yeah, none of us really expected it, but we were all kind of extremely pleased and happy that the nation kind of took us under

DOI: 10.1057/9781137480323.0010

their wing, so to speak, and yeah, we were kind of overwhelmed with the amount of coverage that we did get, and hopefully that'll continue, really.

Cassie agreed that the amount of media coverage they had received during the Olympics had been surprising:

> There was a lot of media coverage regarding the women's team being in the Olympics, I think that was, you obviously kind of expect that, but in terms of the attendances and the newspaper coverage and television coverage, I don't think anybody expected it to be as big as what it was, I think that was a good thing, as we were going on in the tournament we gained a lot more supporters as we went on. Women's football was right up there as one of the highlights of probably the Olympics.

Liz did not feel that being under a media spotlight was intrusive or overwhelming; instead, she welcomed the opportunity to speak to the media, and felt that her teammates felt the same:

> I think we were just really happy for the papers to be putting women's football in them, really, you don't see it very often so it was very nice to have, to have so many back pages, and within the papers as well, just covered with women's football, and also women's sport in general, which was amazing to see at the Olympics, really.

Media coverage going forward

So leading on from this, athletes were very clear that London 2012 had provided a great opportunity for women's sport and had demonstrated the interest in it and the justification for future media coverage. Cassie was optimistic that the women's football team's success during the Olympics was now acting as a springboard for more media coverage of and more supporters attending the FAWSL:

> I knew that we'd get a lot more supporters, averaging over the whole of the WSL games, but I think it was more England games that took a lot more people to come and watch, which was good for us to go and play in front of 5, 6,000 on a Wednesday afternoon in Walsall, I think it was, but I think in terms of attendances, attendances have gone up, definitely bigger. I think the way forward is probably media as in newspapers and letting people know when our games are, especially when the games are on the telly you tend to find a lot more people do watch them than you'd probably expect. We've got so much support from ESPN and BBC, it's obviously a step in

DOI: 10.1057/9781137480323.0010

the right direction...I think obviously the Olympics has done wonders, especially for women's football, and it just shows the support that we've got from the BBC, and they've obviously committed to showing the highlights shows of the WSL now, and England in Europe qualifiers, the European Championships are going to be televised, so I think the more that they're publicised, the more people will watch, and I think it's brilliant for us, and I think everybody's like really glad that they've put the support there.

She admitted, though, that although TV coverage was improving, the print media still lagged behind:

Yeah, I mean, it's a little bit disappointing, but to be honest you're never really going to be able to compete with men's football, I mean, the amount of money that they bring in, and that's what sells the papers, isn't it, really? But even if it's just even a little bit, if you're reading the paper, you'll read it if it's there, kind of thing, so it's a bit frustrating in that sense, but in comparison to a few years ago, there was nothing at all, whereas now, even if it's just a little column it'll be better for us.

Cassie's attitude is very pragmatic; indeed, Ian Prior, the sports editor of the supposedly liberal *Guardian*, admitted in 2013 that the coverage in his part of the newspaper would always be dominated by men's football:

It's really easy to cover women's sports during the Olympics...Everyone wants to read about Jessica Ennis. It's easy when Wimbledon comes along. But beyond that, it comes down to spending time and money to cater to a very small audience. We get flak for not covering women's rugby, cricket and football enough, but it's expensive to cover and the level of interest makes it hard to justify. (*Guardian*, 2013)

The same article pointed out: 'About 50% of the *Guardian's* sports coverage is devoted to football (played by men). And that figure would be even higher, [Prior] says, if editors were entirely governed by market forces: probably 75% of resources and coverage would go to football and 25% to everything else.'

This kind of attitude means that women's sport is presented in ways that will presumably appease the 'market forces' – by showing the sportswomen primarily as 'women' rather than 'athletes'. Cassie was also honest about the downsides of the media coverage, and discussed some of the features that had been run which focused on players' looks rather than their sporting achievements:

I think that's what we're trying to change a bit, the media now, we are actually professional athletes, we are trying to sway towards that instead of

DOI: 10.1057/9781137480323.0010

being dolled up. Yeah, I'm girly and I do shopping or get your hair done or stuff like that, but when I play football, I play football, I'm a footballer, so I think it's just gaining people's respect that you're in a football kit, you just want to play football, it doesn't mean that you're not girly or you do other things outside of football, but I can understand it's frustrating because as players it does get a little bit frustrating.

As suggested at the outset of this chapter, the sportswomen were very aware of their positioning as 'role models' by the media and by governing authorities, and got involved with community outreach work, and significantly, Liz felt that the media coverage during the Olympics had changed the children's responses to her and her teammates:

They all remember the Brazil game, they all know about women's football, which is very nice to see, kind of, a lot of them remember Steph's [Steph Houghton's] goal, so yeah, it's really nice to see, and I think a lot of kids went to the Brazil game as well, which is really nice to see, so, yeah, it has been quite a big difference, not just in terms of women's football, because that's been massive, but also just the amount of excitement that's based around the Olympics... it's just so nice to see kids being inspired by sport, really, and hopefully we can continue with that as well.

Cassie had similar feelings, stressing the importance of good media coverage in order to establish herself and her colleagues as role models:

I think especially I consider myself kind of a little bit like an ambassador for the game, and anything I'm asked to do I'll happily do it. If that helps promote the sport, then it helps promote the sport, but I think you're giving the young girls an opportunity to look up to someone, or a team, it's definitely good to get it out there in the papers, on television as much as possible, and I'd love to be one of them people, one of the girls that they look up to and try to aspire to be, and try and be as professional as possible by doing as much for the game as I can.

Women's football on social media

One of the ways in which this role as 'ambassador' has been formalised is with the FAWSL's 'digital ambassador' plan, where each club nominates one player to take the lead in communicating with fans via social media. Cassie describes it thus:

I think it's something new and people actually did catch on to it when we launched it, it was brilliant. I think it's more of a responsibility to help your

DOI: 10.1057/9781137480323.0010

club and to try and attract people to the games and just basically outlay the information as much as possible via Twitter and via Facebook and there's opportunities where we'll do random question and answers with some of the girls. They're just a little bit more real, whereas I know that a lot of the male footballers' Twitter feeds are done by the agent, or brothers, or whoever, kind of thing, it's nice to be able to read all the actual messages and say, 'Oh, congratulations' or whatever, and somebody wants a happy birthday wish, something like that, it just makes you become a lot more approachable to people, who recognise that it's the real you, really.

This project will be discussed in more detail in the following chapter, but it is worth highlighting here to show the amount of responsibility FAWSL players have in promoting their own game.

Cultural impact of female footballers

FAWSL players are also taking an increasingly prominent role in cultural and societal discourses. Casey Stoney, the former England captain, gave an interview to the BBC in early 2014 stating that she is lesbian and in a relationship. The media reaction was overwhelmingly positive; indeed, there was significantly more mainstream attention paid to this story and Stoney's new position as an LGBTQ role model than there has been to her performances for Arsenal in the FAWSL since. Of course, this incident can indeed be interpreted as another encouraging example of the potential for female footballers to use their increased media attention as a power for good, as the players quoted in this chapter suggest in their efforts to promote sporting participation and their adoption of the position of 'role model'.

However, as the players quoted in this chapter also observe, it remains that the pressure for female athletes – particularly those in the public eye, which elite women footballers are now more than ever – to conform to normative discourses of female (hetero)sexuality, maintaining the restrictive silences around the topic.

Conclusion

Women's sport still has limited coverage; and the FAWSL, despite its fanfare, has not as yet managed to gain a significant proportion of the sports pages. However, it is still relatively early days in the FAWSL's life cycle; perhaps it

DOI: 10.1057/9781137480323.0010

is worth noting here that the elite men's leagues, so dominant in English sports media, have been established for a century and a half.

Yet it is worth noting that the FAWSL strategy and its work with media partners seems rather patchy to say the least. Despite the excellent coverage during the Olympics, this has not been matched since, with domestic games aired on the BBC, ESPN and BT Sport (the latter two of which require a special channel subscription and are far less well established than the well-known and mainstream Sky Sports channels). Because of the lack of publicity for the FAWSL, those wishing to watch the games already have to be aware that they are scheduled and where they might be aired, creating a feel of 'preaching to the converted'. The major issue facing the FAWSL is, clearly, bringing women's football to an audience that is not already invested in it.

It is perhaps unsurprising that our evidence shows that athletes themselves take responsibility for raising their own profile and the profile of their teams, often via social media. However, it is also important to stress that the footballers are very aware of the importance of promoting a positive image not just to secure their own media profiles and to attract more fans to the sport but a desire to inspire young fans.

Notes

1 John Terry is the current Chelsea FC and former England captain, a strong, physical defender who is commended for displaying commitment, passion and vigour, strongly symbolising the dominance of masculinity in football (see for example BBC, 2006). These attributes can be understood to represent the 'ultimate' hegemonic masculinity in football. However, his reputation has been questioned, having faced numerous allegations of gambling, cheating, drinking and fighting, alongside a suspension for racism, leading some to question the appropriateness of John Terry for the position of captain, a position with significant role model responsibilities. See for example http://bleacherreport. com/articles/1350158-john-terry-ban-why-the-chelsea-defender-deserves-a-harsher-suspension.

2 Kelly Smith is perhaps the most successful current English women's football player, with a national and international media profile unlike any other English player (Williams, 2003). She played professionally in the USA in the well-advanced college structure and the professional WUSA and WPS leagues. Between US contracts she played in England for Arsenal where she currently plays as of 2014 (Williams, 2003; http://www.football-england.com/arsenal_ladies_fc.html).

DOI: 10.1057/9781137480323.0010

6
Public Reaction to the FAWSL

Abstract: *This chapter looks at the broad fan engagement with the two-division FAWSL, and suggests that fan reaction, particularly to controversies, has been vociferous, yet this has still been relatively limited. Further, this is not reflected in mainstream media coverage; this chapter puts forward some potential explanations for this. It also looks at the reception of the media coverage of the FAWSL, examining the televised games on BT Sport, the newspaper reports from the mainstream media and the 'specialised' media for women's football, primarily the content of small-scale publications such as* She Kicks.

Dunn, Carrie and Joanna Welford. *Football and the FA Women's Super League: Structure, Governance and Impact.* Basingstoke: Palgrave Macmillan, 2015. DOI: 10.1057/9781137480323.0011.

DOI: 10.1057/9781137480323.0011

Introduction

As the previous chapter emphasised, women's football has long been a minority sport in England, and one of the aims of the FAWSL has been to bring it to a broader audience. This chapter reflects on how successful they have been so far. This chapter also suggests that fan reaction, particularly to controversies, has been vociferous, yet this has still been relatively limited – and not reflected in mainstream media coverage. We discuss this phenomenon and also put forward some potential explanations for this.

WSL launch and fan engagement

When the WSL launched, the FA's briefing paper (2010) expressed its wish to create an 'exciting and competitive league', and promised that its initial major focus would be to raise the profile of the league. At that point, they had secured a broadcast partnership with ESPN to air selected games and highlights throughout the season, and described the broadcaster as having an 'important role in helping to support the PR plans'.

They promised that 'spectator numbers; TV broadcast numbers; [and] how far we have raised profile with existing and new media' would be three of the key measures of the league's success. They gave an outline of the WSL's developing marketing and communications plan, to operate in conjunction with the clubs and their own individual plans.

Reflection on WSL's first season

The FA's official reflection on the inaugural season was enthusiastic, listing: "In the league's first season, attendances increased to a league wide average of 550 per game, there has been week in week out TV coverage with 17 WSL shows and 6 live games broadcast on ESPN, the league winners were only determined on the final day of the season and our digital following increased significantly with FAWSL social media channels, attracting over 80,000 followers. English players continue to return from the US as standards in England both on and off the pitch improve and more semi-professional players are earning a living from the game."

DOI: 10.1057/9781137480323.0011

They went on: "Average attendances in 2011 were 550 per match, with many clubs, attracting over 1,000 fans at higher-profile fixtures running through the summer months. Four FAWSL clubs broke their record attendance figures, Bristol (1,138), Chelsea (2,510), Everton (1,135) and Birmingham (824). Compared to previous attendances when clubs were playing in the winter FA Women's Premier League, the number of fans attending games has increased significantly (604%)."

In terms of media coverage, their statement reiterated that the status quo would continue: "A full review has taken place with ESPN and the agreement for 2012 is to provide at least the same amount of coverage. Both the FA and ESPN were pleased with the 2011 viewing figures for live matches: the peak figures were on a par with the Scottish Premier League viewing figures. We can also confirm that the FAWSL weekly highlights show will continue in 2012. This will be a 30-minute show, broadcast at 7pm, Tuesday evenings on ESPN.

"Media coverage online and in consumer and lifestyle press has increased in 2011, as did media coverage in the local areas surrounding the eight FAWSL clubs. This has helped increase overall awareness of the FAWSL, which peaked at 55% amongst football fans in 2011."

The impact of London 2012

As the previous chapter described, the second season of the FAWSL was interrupted by a mid-season break to allow players to participate in the 2012 Olympic Games. Although Team GB's men's football team consisted of an under-21-eligible squad, the women's team (coached by then England manager Hope Powell) comprised senior players from the representative international teams (although in practice the vast majority of the players were English with two Scots, and one Northern Irish player named as a standby). All but three of the 19 squad players belonged to clubs from the FAWSL. (The squad limit was 18 but Dunia Susi of England and Chelsea was called up after Ifeoma Dieke of Scotland and Vittsjo was injured in the second match.)

Team GB enjoyed a highly successful Games, beating New Zealand, Cameroon and Brazil in the group stage, but being knocked out by Canada in the quarterfinals. Perhaps more significantly for the future of the women's game in England, the attendance at matches was impressive. A total of 70,584 people attended England's match against Brazil, hosted

DOI: 10.1057/9781137480323.0011

at Wembley Stadium, which the FA's later press release described as 'the largest crowd to watch a women's game in this country since 1920'. The final, again at Wembley and contested by USA and Japan, attracted 80,203 fans to the ground as well as a sizeable TV audience in the UK; again, the FA's press materials gave the figures as 3.9 million viewers at its peak. The same FA survey (issued by press release in August 2012) stated that almost 70% of the 1,000 people they surveyed would consider going to watch a live women's game – an increase of 15% since before the Olympics.

Digital ambassadors and the importance of social media

The FA established from the start that one of the great lessons they could learn from the US experience of elite women's football leagues was their excellent and engaging use of new media. It is of course possible to argue that social media is a relatively simple choice of outlet for engagement for a league and its clubs operating within strict financial restraints, but it is perhaps more useful to consider the FA's defined target audience of younger people, who rely more on social and new media for their information than on the traditional mainstream press.

In their 2011 reflection on the first WSL season, the FA praised the 'significant effect [of social media] on the amount of potential fans' available to clubs, announcing that over 80,000 fans had signed up to follow a player, club or the league itself on Facebook and Twitter over the course of the season. This coincided with their first major themed promotional campaign, 'Call the Shots', inviting fans to vote for the player of the match, select music played on match days, and which players would speak to the fans after each game. In season two, as the previous chapter noted, the FA launched an innovative Digital Ambassador programme intended to increase the connection between fans and players.

FAWSL expansion and engagement

After two seasons of the FAWSL and a broadcast partnership with ESPN, the FA announced in May 2013 that it would be working with BT Sport going forward to air WSL matches as well as covering Cup matches and internationals.

DOI: 10.1057/9781137480323.0011

Their press release declared: 'As an exclusive partner to The FAWSL, BT will have the opportunity to reach a broad and growing demographic, with a fan base and appeal that is increasing all the time. With an integrated broadcast and marketing strategy, BT will be able to communicate with customers through a national programme with genuine local relevance and make a real and measurable difference to the progression of the sport.' Stuart Turner, the FA's commercial director, described BT as 'the perfect partner to help take the game forward over the next four years', while the head of BT Sport, Simon Green, said that women's sport was a 'major focus' of their programming.

It is unsurprising, then, that the FAWSL's 2013 brochure inviting applications for the new two-division set-up boasted of the greater media exposure available to participating clubs. Not only that, but they also made it clear that although the broadcast footage (or 'commercial in-camera inventory') is owned by the FA and allocated to FAWSL partners, 40% of it is given back to clubs who can sell it on or use it in their own commercial partnerships. The need for appropriate partnerships is a focus of the FA's documentation, which mentions the FAWSL's 'new and enthusiastic family audience' and opportunities to work with companies 'for whom the men's game is not necessarily the right fit'.

As we have seen, the FA were keen to stress the attendance increases for the WSL compared to the previous top flight of women's football, claiming there was a rise of 604%. Obviously, this is not a fair comparison – the 2010–2011 season ran on the winter league cycle, and, as the FA have pointed out repeatedly, women's football has been overshadowed by the men's game as well as people's own playing and coaching engagements.

However, they also indicated that their original research showed a bigger interest in women's football, claiming that since London 2012, 69% of the British population would go and see a women's football match (up 15% from pre-Olympics), and that 36% of respondents were interested in the FAWSL (compared to 40% who were interested in the men's Championship, i.e. the second tier, and 32% in the Europa League, second-tier men's European club competition).

Media and marketing for the FAWSL going forward is key. The 2013 club development plan guidelines specified that clubs wanting a place in the top flight needed to have 'a Match Promotion/Marketing Officer' in place by the start of 2014, who needed to be approved by the FA, who would also offer financial support and training. This staffing requirement

DOI: 10.1057/9781137480323.0011

was not applicable to the clubs wanting a place in FAWSL2, but they were encouraged to take advantage of money from the Club Development Fund to improve their communications and promotions activity.

Clubs also needed to provide a commercial, marketing and media plan for the next two seasons as part of the club development plan, which would 'demonstrate how a club will grow and retain its spectator base, develop its profile in its catchment area, and build its commercial revenue'. These plans had to include objectives for growing the fanbase, plans for communicating with fans and the wider local community, a budget for these activities, and information about commercial partnerships and sponsorships.

Of course, the FA are hoping that this increased promotional activity will also increase clubs' attendances, and as such they also built into their application process a set of target figures indicating regular spectator attendance projections (Table 6.1).

The applications from clubs needed to demonstrate that these targets were achievable (although the FA did add that a promoted club would have its own amended targets rather than being expected to keep pace with the long-established clubs), providing data about the core and average supporter base for the previous two seasons as well as information about why support was not currently higher. Again, significantly, the FA were quick to point out that newly created clubs did not need to provide these data.

The breadth of media coverage

The 2013 announcement that BT Sport would be an official partner of women's football going forward followed increased coverage from the

TABLE 6.1   *Projected minimum attendances for FAWSL clubs*

Season	FAWSL1 club projected minimum attendance	FAWSL2 club projected minimum attendance
2014	550	250
2015	600	300
2016	700	350
2017	800	400

DOI: 10.1057/9781137480323.0011

BBC. When England reached the quarterfinals of the Women's World Cup in 2011, the BBC were not initially intending to show it live, but following public outcry they changed their mind, screening it on BBC2. Since then, the BBC have worked to improve their coverage of women's football; they now have an editorial lead for women's sport, who takes an overview on all the issues, and covering women's sport also fits in neatly to their public service remit. They now regularly show home England internationals live, and have a monthly women's football show.

However, one of the potential problems of these 'partnerships' is the erosion of journalistic independence. There has been a failure to address controversies in the game, such as the reasons for Hope Powell's departure as England manager (when the equivalent in the men's game would have engendered many scores of column inches and hours of broadcast coverage), or, indeed, the selection of the WSL clubs in each division (as discussed in the previous chapters). Both parties are heavily reliant on each other, and as such there is little space for dealing with topics or events that are more controversial. This has, in fact, been a historical problem in coverage of women's football in England. Typically, there have been very few journalists covering women's football regularly, meaning that the output has been relatively narrow and reflecting these limited interests.

The FA's 2010 briefing document recognised this problem, but only in terms of the limited amount of coverage, criticising 'most of the media' for not taking 'a considered interest in women's football, other than when the national team does well at a major tournament' and bemoaning the lack of 'momentum or consistency in the media profile for the game'. Although this may be true, it does not recognise the difficulty that is now being encountered: guaranteeing more media coverage does not necessarily guarantee better, more thoughtful, broader media coverage. The emphasis on commercial partnerships where all involved parties stand to benefit – such as the broadcast deals – does not take into account the possibility that women's football could encourage independent journalism as well, and benefit from this.

FAWSL matches are scheduled for Sunday afternoons (i.e. not on Saturdays, when many football fans will be at men's matches, and not Sunday mornings, when others will be playing) and Thursday evenings. Although the league is scheduled as a summer competition, the traditional British autumn–spring set-up still has an impact; clubs from all over England still compete for the FA Women's Cup (a competition which includes FAWSL members) from September to April. Thus so far the FAWSL season has been planned with a mid-season break; in 2011 this allowed space for players to take part in the Women's World Cup, in 2012 the Olympics, and in 2013 the European Championships.

This may be a sensible set-up, but this gap in competition does not contribute to an ongoing continuous narrative, one of the established requirements for a story to be selected for news coverage (cf. Galtung and Ruge, 1965; Schulz, 1982). Coverage of the FAWSL is inconsistent partially by necessity; the mid-season break built into the FAWSL means that there are several weeks every summer without fixtures, requiring two separate build-ups per season, reminding the viewer of the league's existence. Reporting from FAWSL matches is still limited; national newspapers and websites tend to publish round-ups of the action rather than in-depth match reports. There is also a heavy reliance on agency reporters and freelancers along with club and league press releases instead of using staff to cover matches; despite the FA's high-profile trumpeting of its commercial partnerships and its broadcast agreements, there has so far been little sustained increase of regular match-day journalism around the WSL.

As might perhaps be expected, the lack of mainstream print and online coverage for women's football has led to specialist publications and websites setting themselves up to cover FAWSL matches. SheKicks is probably the best-known magazine and website for women's football in the UK, and was established originally in 1996, having previously been known as On the Ball and Fair Game. However, such a specialist publication still relies on limited funds and staff, meaning they too rely on voluntary contributions and information from clubs where possible.

Conclusion: public knowledge

The FAWSL has a much higher profile now than any other top-flight women's league in England in recent times. That is not in dispute. What we question, really, is the quality and utility of the coverage it receives and whether the FAWSL could be better reported and esteemed than it is. We have pointed out that independent journalistic coverage of the FAWSL is very limited indeed, with too much reliance on the coverage of 'broadcast partners' and also the PR staff of clubs and the FA itself. As many journalism scholars have discussed in relation to news, the move

DOI: 10.1057/9781137480323.0011

towards reliance on PR is a dangerous one; it means a lack of independence and objectivity, and a shift towards 'churnalism' – the same output from all outlets.

It can easily be surmised – and we are suggesting – that despite the FA's eagerness to capitalise on lucrative and high-profile commercial partnerships to establish media coverage, this does not necessarily encourage long-term improved media coverage across all platforms. We are not, of course, suggesting that this is a simple problem that can be solved purely by the FA; it is an endemic issue across women's sport, as our previous chapters indicate. However, although press releases and public-facing publications from the FA are inevitably going to report the optimistic, we would like to urge caution and propose that there needs to be some long-term consideration of how the FAWSL and elite women's football in England can and should be covered across all media – not just live broadcasts of games.

DOI: 10.1057/9781137480323.0011

7
The Future of the FAWSL

Abstract: *This chapter highlights that as the first football league of this licence-driven style in Europe, the FAWSL is an important site for examining the impact of this league structure. The first four seasons of the FAWSL are discussed and evaluated against its own original objectives. It speculates that attempts by the FA to promote gender equity may in fact be having the opposite effect with the imposition of the FAWSL two-division structure and the negative impacts increased professionalisation can bring. It discusses potential future directions and amendments to the existing set-up.*

Dunn, Carrie and Joanna Welford. *Football and the FA Women's Super League: Structure, Governance and Impact.* Basingstoke: Palgrave Macmillan, 2015.
DOI: 10.1057/9781137480323.0012.

Introduction

This chapter returns to some of the debates at the outset of the book in considering what impact the FAWSL has had on women's football. Chapter 1 introduced the context in which the FAWSL was launched – one that uncomfortably combined increasing participation rates with the continued marginalisation of the sport. It is important to consider whether things have changed since the inception of the first semi-professional football league for women, and whether the aims that the FA set out for the WSL have been achieved. Finally, we ask what the future might hold for semi-professional football for women in England.

How has the FAWSL fared against its original aims and objectives?

The early FAWSL promotional material set out a number of aims and objectives for the league specifically and the game generally, and these were added to in later documents looking further to the future. The main objectives of the FAWSL, amalgamated from the various documents released before and during the WSL so far, are

- ▶ to increase the competitiveness and quality of elite women's football;
- ▶ to attract and retain England's most talented players;
- ▶ to give better opportunities to elite players;
- ▶ to strengthen the elite player pathway;
- ▶ to improve the national team;
- ▶ to increase fan numbers and improve the fan experience;
- ▶ to increase the profile of women's football (media exposure and investment);
- ▶ to increase participation at all levels of the sport;
- ▶ to improve the standard of facilities available to women – with the Game Changer (The FA, 2012a) document suggesting that clubs 'own modern, family and fan friendly home grounds at the heart of the community'.

It is important to evaluate whether these aims and objectives have been met – or, considering the infancy of this league, are on their way to being met – looking at but also beyond the promotional material produced by

DOI: 10.1057/9781137480323.0012

the FA. It is outside of the scope of this chapter to look in detail at all of these objectives, so a selection will be discussed and evaluated using evidence available in the public domain.

1   To increase the competitiveness and quality of elite women's football

Judging whether this aim has been met is very difficult, as quality is a very subjective term. Competitiveness however can be judged to an extent. As discussed in Chapter 1, the Women's Premier League was dominated by Arsenal in the decade prior to the start of the FAWSL, with Everton consistently finishing in second place between 2006 and 2010. A major reason for introducing the new format league was to challenge this dominance and foster the spread of playing talent across more of the top clubs.

It took some time for this to happen. Arsenal won the inaugural FAWSL season as well as the Continental (league) Cup and FA Cup. The year 2012 saw a similar story, with Arsenal again winning the Continental Cup and the FAWSL, this time by eight points, but failing to make the FA Cup final where Birmingham City beat Chelsea to lift the trophy. There may have been some concern by this point (by fans if not the FA) over whether the FAWSL had indeed increased the competitiveness of women's football. The year 2013 however finally saw a shift in the balance, reflecting that this was not going to be an immediate change. Liverpool – who had by this time solidified their partnership with the men's club, allowing most of the team to train full-time – won the FAWSL by five points, but the penultimate game of the season against Bristol Academy was the title decider, giving an exciting end to the season. Arsenal finished third, hindered by having three points deducted for fielding an ineligible player, but again won the Continental Cup and regained the FA Cup (which they then won again in 2014). At the time of writing, Liverpool had just retained their title on goal difference – the final day saw the title change hands as any of three teams were in the position to win the 2014 FAWSL1. Neither of the 'new' clubs to FAWSL1 – Manchester City and Notts County, both with strong financial backing from their male club partner – have been title contenders in their first season. Manchester City did however win the 2014 Continental Cup, so the three available trophies were all won by different clubs.

DOI: 10.1057/9781137480323.0012

It would be hard to argue that the competitiveness of the elite women's football has not increased over the first phase of the FAWSL. Arsenal no longer dominate, and perhaps more encouragingly, they have not been simply replaced by one different dominant club. Some clubs undoubtedly have bigger budgets than others, but this does not appear to be a precursor to success at this moment in time. It would be surprising, however, if this did not change; new clubs who have significant financial investment, particularly Manchester City, may take some time to translate money into success but there is always the concern that differing budgets even within FAWSL1 will start to play more of a role as the league develops.

2   To give better opportunities to elite players

When the FAWSL was first launched, only the 16 centrally contracted England players at the time were paid (a modest £16,000 a year) for playing football (Williams, 2013). The FAWSL has undoubtedly allowed more women to earn through football, although as clubs do not divulge playing budgets and other financial information, it is difficult to estimate just how many earn a wage purely from playing the game. The FA has set a £20,000 salary cap with each club able to pay four players above this amount, and for this wage, players are likely to spend time on community programmes and other ambassadorial work. The more restrictive salary cap is the current limit of 40% of the club turnover to be spent on player wages. The minimum operating budget for FAWSL1 clubs is £140,000 (£70,000 club matched with £70,000 FA funding) and 40% of this figure is £56,000, not enough to even pay three players £20,000. To pay the minimum 16-player first team squad an average of £20,000 each – 4 players above the cap balanced with several below – would cost clubs £320,000 a year, therefore requiring a turnover of £800,000. Whether the better-funded clubs have access to this type of money or not, it is clear that even if a small proportion of female players are now earning a living playing the game, the majority will still have to supplement small earnings with other jobs. Of course, the FAWSL is and was always intended to be semi-professional, and there are no plans to drop the 'semi' from the description, so it is not expected that all players will receive a full-time wage. But the figures do raise some questions about how much it is possible to earn purely through football, and therefore

DOI: 10.1057/9781137480323.0012

how realistic the idea of 'full-time training' is to many clubs who have a limited operating budget.

Although very few female players can now earn a living from playing football without needing to work, this is an improvement for them. Some wage is better than no wage; 'some professional players' is better than 'no professional players'. But accepting this is a dangerous proclamation, as it can over-emphasise the gains made and underemphasise what is still to be done. The gap between the salaries of top female and top male football players is amongst the widest of any sport, and works to legitimise their inferiority.

3   To increase fan numbers and improve the fan experience

As noted earlier, after the first WSL season, the FA reported that average attendances of 550 and peak attendances of well over 1,000 represented a 604% increase on previous WPL figures (The FA, 2012a). The Women's Sport and Fitness Foundation celebrate that this was higher than for any men's football league below the Conference (WSFF, 2011), but as Conference football represents steps five and six of the male football pyramid, and the FAWSL has no competition from men's football for most of this season, these figures must be put in perspective. Attendances over the first three seasons all averaged between 500 and 600.

The year 2014 has seen an increase on the previous three seasons. These figures are helped by two of the best three attended clubs, Notts County and Manchester City, replacing the two clubs with the lowest attendances over the previous three seasons (Doncaster Belles and Lincoln). FAWSL2, however, has seen some particularly low figures in its first season.

Attendance figures for FA Cup finals since the start of the FAWSL are interesting. This may not be of concern to the FA, as their focus is on the league rather than the cup, but FA Cup final attendances over the past four seasons have been nowhere near their peak in 2007–2009. Less than 5,000 watched Arsenal beat Bristol Academy in 2013, the lowest in over a decade. Playing a final featuring two Southern clubs in Doncaster may have contributed to this, although the required travelling did not stop almost 25,000 watching Arsenal and Charlton contest the final in Nottingham in 2007. So although FAWSL attendances (in the top division

DOI: 10.1057/9781137480323.0012

at least) are what the FA considers as healthy, it is interesting that there has been a decrease in FA Cup final attendances – the game that used to be the flagship event in the women's football calendar.

Improvements to the fan experience are again difficult to judge. Social media interaction has been a major part of the strategy to improve the accessibility of players, allowing them to communicate directly with fans and therefore improve the fan experience (WSFF, 2011). Those attending FAWSL games are likely to experience pre-match entertainment, a fan zone for families, music and interaction with players. This is very much aimed at the specific target audience of 9–15-year-old girls and their families. This change could be perceived in two ways – the FA are encouraging clubs to provide a football 'experience' that goes beyond the game, but conversely, this entertainment detracts from the football.

4   To increase the profile of women's football

The FA stresses that women's football is now much more marketable under the FAWSL brand, allowing key sponsorship partnerships to be developed (WSFF, 2014). The FAWSL is used by the Women's Sport and Fitness Foundation as a successful case study of 'creative collaboration' between a governing body, a broadcaster and sponsor businesses (WSFF, 2011). The DCMS in their 2014 report on Women in Sport also praise the FA for its work so far in increasing the profile of the women's game, particularly in securing sponsorship partners and broadcasting rights, but suggest that they could do more.

Television exposure has been a focus of the FA to increase the profile of the game, and Chapter 5 discusses this in more detail. Audience figures for the six matches shown live on Eurosport in 2011 were higher than expected (The FA, 2012c). BT Sport acquired the rights to the FAWSL for the 2014–2018 period, with 14 live games broadcast across the 2014 season. However, both Eurosport and BT Sport are subscription-only channels, so are not available free to the general public. They also hold a much smaller market share than Sky Sports who have been conspicuously absent when it comes to reporting women's football, having been criticised for cutting the live transmission before the end of the 2012 FA Cup final (Gayle, 2012) and not featuring the Euro 2013 fixtures (WSC, 2013a). The FAWSL has a YouTube channel showing highlights of games, and has a strong digital media presence. Whilst this media strategy has increased the presence of women's football across different formats, it is questionable whether this reaches beyond the existing fanbase. The lack of terrestrial coverage means that the casual sports consumer is unlikely to come across women's football by chance, which could significantly limit the reach of the sport.

The BBC has also been criticised for a lack of support for women's football. For the 2013 European Championships, England games were shown live on BBC3[1] and received viewing figures that were at around 1 million higher than average for the time slot (DCMS, 2014); but even so not all of their 2015 World Cup qualifying matches were shown live. Since 2013 the BBC have aired 'The Women's Football Show', with eight episodes across the FAWSL season, although for the first year it was aired on BBC2 at varying times between 11.00pm and 1.00am, inaccessible for the target audience of 9–15-year-old girls and unlikely to be stumbled upon by others (for the 2014 season it has been moved to a 7.00pm slot, but on BBC3).

5   To increase participation at all levels of the sport

The Game Changer document stated that the 2008–2012 period, encompassing the build up to launch and first two seasons of the FAWSL, saw an increase in the numbers of female coaches and referees, with the number of registered girls' and adult teams also rising (The FA, 2012a). There has however been a gradual decline in the number of people (male and female) playing football since 2005, exposing problems across the grassroots level of the sport (Gibson, 2014).

Although numbers of female coaches and referees may well be increasing, there is an unsurprising indication that women and girls in these roles still struggle to be accepted, and often qualify in male-dominated environments (Fielding-Lloyd and Meân, 2011; Norman, 2014). Refereeing remains a particular problem; the very small number that have broken into the elite level of male football have experienced sexist attitudes[2] and those that participate at the amateur level have also been exposed to hostile treatment (Forbes et al., 2014). Quoting increased participation figures, particularly in these non-playing roles, gives only a partial view of the reality. Increasing numbers in itself does little for integration in any aspect of society, yet is so often seen as a sign of success in sport. Once qualified, how do female referees and coaches experience

DOI: 10.1057/9781137480323.0012

football? Are they given opportunities to progress? Are they accepted? The minimal research done in this area suggests that beyond the figures, the situation for female referees and coaches in football remains far from equitable.

Accurate and up-to-date participation figures to compare numbers over the past decade are difficult to obtain and compare, as different surveys measure different levels of participation. Sport England's Active People Survey[3] is conducted quarterly and reported annually, and is most often referred to when adult participation figures are used (The FA and the WSFF use these statistics). Figures for 2007–2013 show a gradual decline in the number of 16+ females playing football once a week since 2009 (Table 7.1).

The largest drop in participation has been the two seasons since the launch of the FAWSL. Although these figures only represent the 16+ age group, this is a concerning trend. Figures for the first and second quarter of 2014 do show an increase, but as these do not cover the whole year, they may be unreflective of the yearly figure.

The drop in women playing football post-16 is a concern, and suggests that the aim to increase participation at all levels is not currently being met. Again, we need to look beyond the figures, and ask questions. This is essential if there has in fact been a drop in female football participation. Why has this happened? The FA spends a bulk of their women's football budget on the elite level – the FAWSL and aspects of the talent pathway, such as Centres of Excellence. Girls' football is funded alongside other grassroots initiatives. This leaves the bulk of the women's football pyramid – adult players outside of the FAWSL – as largely absent from funding priorities. Critics of the FA's funding strategy have argued that women's football clubs are folding at an alarming rate and are not being replaced.[4]

TABLE 7.1   *Number of females aged 16+ playing football once a week*

Year	Number playing	Change on previous year
2007–2008	146,800	
2008–2009	156,300	+9,500 (+6.5%)
2009–2010	151,200	−5,100 (−3.4%)
2010–2011	144,500	−6,700 (−4.4%)
2011–2012	128,700	−15,800 (−11.0%)
2012–2013	115,700	−13,000 (−10.1%)

Note: Up- to- date figures available for analysis at http://activepeople.sportengland.org/.

DOI: 10.1057/9781137480323.0012

The wider impact of the FAWSL

Barring the final point about increasing participation, the section above considered the impact that the FAWSL has had on the elite level of the sport. However the biggest impact of the FAWSL might not be at the top level, but in fact be felt throughout the rest of the game. Extending our examination of women's football beyond the FAWSL exposes the major concern over this experimental league: it is focused solely on the FAWSL. Although this might sound an obvious and unavoidable conclusion, it is important to discuss how the injection of funds, resources and infrastructure in the new elite leagues has reverberated across the rest of the female football arena. Two areas will be used to illustrate this – the rest of the adult football pyramid, and wider understandings of women playing football.

What about the leagues below the FAWSL?

The Game Changer strategy (The FA, 2012a) sets out its elite focus from the very start. Although its predecessor, the 2008–2012 Women's Football Strategy, did not feature a player in a top domestic or international team until page 16, the Game changer cover picture is of England players and only 2 of the 13 pages contain pictures that could be considered as representing the grassroots or participatory level of the sport. The two brochures are very different in appearance, with the 2008–2012 strategy presenting an accessible, holistic image and Game Changer reflecting a more polished, professional finish. The 2008–2012 strategy still has a focus on the elite level, as it introduces the FAWSL for the first time, but it is perhaps eased in more gently. By the Game Changer document, the FA has narrowed its focus to the elite and made no apology about it. Of the four key commitments outlined, the first three are all about the elite game. At the bottom of the list, number four, is increasing participation – ever-present in any FA material. Targeting the elite level as a priority is presumably in the hope that by intervening at this level, positive changes will filter down the rest of the pyramid.

Game Changer outlines changes to the football pyramid, but only at the top. The Women's Premier League, now tier three of the pyramid, which must support the FAWSL if there is any intention of integration with the rest of the leagues, is not mentioned. And herein lies one of

DOI: 10.1057/9781137480323.0012

the biggest criticisms of the FAWSL – it is disjointed from the rest of the football pyramid which is preventing any benefits from filtering down to the rest of the game. By putting all of the resources into this level, there is a very real concern that a gulf will develop between the FAWSL and 'the rest'. The summer league format already separates it structurally; funding discrepancies may widen the separation in terms of playing ability, and the lack of attention paid particularly to the WPL by the FA has the potential to create a cultural separation, an 'us versus them' mentality if non-WSL clubs feel overlooked. So not only do clubs outside the FAWSL feel that the league has not benefited them, but there are signs that it may be to the detriment of the rest of the pyramid.

In December 2013, following the announcement of the expansion to include FAWSL2, the FA released a statement[5] that outlined its plans for the soon-to-be third tier WPL and beyond. It acknowledged that the 'winter pyramid' as it is now known is vital to support the elite level, and described how the WPL and the Combination leagues (the tier below the WPL) would be combined to form 'The Women's Championship League, supported by The FA'. Funding for the 72 clubs that would make up the Championship would be in the form of an annual £90,000 grant, representing £1250 per club.

WPL clubs responded with dismay at this announcement (despite voting in the changes earlier in the year, although there are suggestions that they were not offered an alternative). A 'Save Our WPL' group was formed, who quickly released a statement outlining their concerns over the future of non-WSL clubs and leagues and demanding a meeting with the FA to discuss a number of issues.[6] Their concerns included how replacing the FA brand with 'supported by the FA' would affect the legitimacy of the league and its appeal to sponsors; that new funding proposals would represent a significant drop in funding from the £145,000 previously split amongst 22 WPL clubs (£6591pa), which would weaken the league rather than strengthen it to support the WSL; and the continued silence on the issue of promotion and relegation between the FAWSL and the former WPL.[7]

Perhaps due to the significant support for the movement – the campaign received a large amount of publicity through social platforms and national media – the FA met with WPL representatives the following month at a Special General Meeting to discuss their concerns. The outcome to the meeting included retaining the FA WPL title and for promotion and relegation to be addressed 'as a matter of urgency'.[8]

DOI: 10.1057/9781137480323.0012

In June 2014 it was announced that from 2016 (following the current 2014–2015 winter season), one WPL club will be promoted into FAWSL2 'providing they meet licencing requirements'.[9] This important caveat is unsurprising, as all other clubs have had to meet these requirements, but it does suggest that in line with the FAWSL precedent, promotion will not be as straightforward as winning the league but will be dependent on a number of off-field factors. It also allows the FA to continue to have the ultimate say over who is included in the FAWSL and who is not. Challenging the FA over the WSL is a brave move by WPL clubs who will ultimately want to be accepted into the league.

It is difficult to not have sympathy with WPL clubs. Some have played in the top flight of women's football in the past ten years; more have played in the second tier, and a number of these have seen their FAWSL applications rejected whilst they move down the women's football pyramid through reasons other than their on-field results. Players with ambition have left to join WSL clubs. Blackburn Rovers, Leeds and Nottingham Forest have all suffered problems since not being included in the original FAWSL (discussed in Chapter 2). The development of the WSL could not benefit everyone. But it is difficult to see how the two sides of the game – the winter and summer pyramids – can truly be integrated in their current format.

What about the impact on women's football more widely?

Chapter 1 discussed the development of women's football in the nineteenth and early twentieth century, concluding that one of the biggest dilemmas facing the sport throughout its early and recent history has been the competition it has faced from the more established male game. The historical struggles faced by women and girls wishing to play football frame the current situation – we are shaped by our pasts, and football is no different. We can now return to this context to examine if anything has changed since the advent of the FAWSL. Whilst the 1993 takeover of women's football by the FA represented a watershed moment in the status that women held in football – no longer were they outsiders, but they were now accepted into the established male structures – the FAWSL arguably represents a more significant step. Not in funding, as discussed later, but in celebrating an aspect of the sport that has been at

DOI: 10.1057/9781137480323.0012

best tolerated and at worst completely excluded throughout the history of their governance. In (finally) committing to a semi-professional league, and making it happen, the governing body of football are promoting their support and commitment to the women's game and its future. But the effect this could have on how the game is perceived is limited, due to what happens when you consider the FAWSL in the context of the rest of the football world. Despite women's football being brought inside the existing structure, it remains very much on the outside in many respects and the FAWSL is arguably strengthening rather than challenging this outsider status. Several aspects can be used to illustrate this.

The FA champions the investment it is currently making in women's football. But the £3 million investment over the first three years (The FA, 2010), and £3.5 million over the next four (The FA, 2012a), does not represent a significant sum of money relative to their turnover or expenditure. The FA, a not-for-profit governing body, reported a turnover of £318 million in 2012, and it invests around £100 million into football each year (The FA, 2012b). The £1 million per year investment in the FAWSL therefore represents 0.31% of their 2012 turnover and 1% of their overall investment in football, 2% of their investment in 'the national game' (anything that is not the 'professional game'). This is not a significant proportion. The DCMS (2014) suggest that greater financial support would increase respect for the women's game. Yes, the FA have been outright with their modest aims, to start small, consider sustainability, and do not want to make the same financial mistakes made by the US professional leagues. But the result is that women's football appears low on their priority list.

Secondly, the summer league structure that has long been one of the most advocated changes to benefit women's football may also be contributing to its inferior position. Moving women's football to the summer would address many issues the women's game faces – wet pitches that are unplayable by Sunday afternoons, competing with men's and boys' teams for facilities, fighting for column inches in the media and spectators in grounds. Logistically, this has brought limited success and created further problems. Pitches are dry in the summer, often no better a playing surface than they are in the winter, and need maintenance in preparation for the winter league. Liverpool Ladies and Everton Ladies currently share a stadium with a 3G (artificial) pitch – ironically, artificial pitches are gaining popularity in football (albeit only in the lower leagues) as the all-weather surface allows year-round participation and prevents

DOI: 10.1057/9781137480323.0012

matches from being postponed. The summer programme has to take a break for women's international tournaments, leaving it disjointed with inconsistent schedules – following a women's team cannot become a weekly habit. It also has to compete with a major men's tournament every two years that provides just as much competition as the Premier League does.

But most importantly, the summer league structure marginalises the women's game. It keeps it outside of what football 'is' to many people in England – a sport played through the autumn, winter and spring, with a break in the summer. Practically, it is scheduled outside of the regular season, but more importantly, culturally it is pushed outside of the football arena. It can be forgotten about whilst people enjoy the World Cup, holidays and barbeques. Yes, summer matches may appeal to some of those who need their football fix. They may go to a match if they have nothing else to do on a Sunday afternoon. But considering the target audience is for the FAWSL is 9–15-year-old girls, they are unlikely to need prising away from Premier League or Football League matches.

Finally, the outsider status is further compounded by the licensing system and the closed league format. This is even more alien to European football than the summer season, and goes against the very traditions of football. Admittedly, female exclusion was also a tradition of football, so not all are in need of celebrating. But the pyramid system is at the very heart of the sport. Football has promotion and relegation; it has teams who grow from and are connected to their communities. For many, it still represents the dream – however slim – that you can start at the bottom and work your way to the top purely on merit. And if your team are relegated, it is because they aren't good enough. Chapter 4 discussed how the fan reaction to licensing in the case of Doncaster Belles and Lincoln City hit this point home. The licensing system is unjust and unfair, and in implementing this in women's football, it can almost be dismissed as an 'alternative' sport. It is again not 'real' football, because 'real' football does not allow clubs to jump leagues, enter at a level that they have not merited with previous performances or be removed from its local community (with the obvious exception of the hugely unpopular decision to allow Wimbledon to be moved to Milton Keynes). It does not allow clubs to be relegated before a season starts because they do not have an appropriate business plan. Alongside the summer league format, the licensing system relegates women's football to something that is not quite football, allowing it to be overlooked and even intentionally ignored by fans of football who

DOI: 10.1057/9781137480323.0012

do not agree with these aspects. These are just the most obvious examples of how the FAWSL separates itself from 'real' football – there are others, such as the use of artificial pitches that aligns the game more closely with recreational football rather than the elite game.

Culturally and structurally, female football remains 'outside' what football is to many, despite integration with the FA and a semi-professional league suggesting that they are now further 'inside' the sport than ever. The 'outsiders on the inside' analogy was proposed by Crosset (1995) in relation to female professional golfers, arguing that the structure and culture of the sport prevents them from being accepted with the golfing world despite their professional status. They were inside the profession but faced constant reminders that they play by slightly different cultural rules, so remained on the outside. It is equally relevant to women in football (Welford, 2008, 2013), from the governance of the game through to the grassroots, and can help to explain why increases in female participation in football have not resulted in gender equity in the sport, or anything close to this. The FAWSL will struggle to overcome the wider issues faced by women's football whilst its inherent features separate it from what 'football' is widely understood to be.

Of course, we acknowledge that the FAWSL is designed to be different from male football structures, to be marketed and even to be celebrated as such. As the WSFF state, the FA wants women's football to be 'a sport distinct and different from men's football rather than its pale imitation' (WSFF, 2011). This is an understandable starting position: women's football cannot compete with men's football for spectators, media coverage, commercial appeal and many other things. It is played differently. It is a different sport. But it is also the same sport. This contradiction is not a new challenge for women's football, and there are no easy answers for how the game should best proceed to carve a space for its own development whilst not ostracising itself from the wider football world.

What the FAWSL has demonstrated is that any attempt by the FA to reconcile this tension – women's football being unable to compete with its male counterpart, but struggling to be accepted as part of the wider game – is focussed purely on the women's game. 'Adding' women, bit by bit, to the football world is believed to lead eventually to an equitable situation. But inclusion does not equal equity; the presence of women is not enough. It is the nature of inclusion that is key, and the experiences of female coaches and officials – still arguably more masculine dominated fields than playing football – highlight this.

DOI: 10.1057/9781137480323.0012

The FAWSL concept is changing women's football to try and improve its situation. But it is the wider male structure and culture of football that is marginalising the women's game – perhaps it is this that needs to be challenged rather than trying to modify the female game to fit it into the men's? The current strategy will never be truly successful because the culture that women are trying to penetrate remains untouched. Changing this culture is of course a huge challenge. Football as a male preserve has such historical strength in European culture, and women's football is still comparably in its infancy. But structurally there are things that could be done that would at least start the ball rolling. The domination of the media by men's football and the lack of female representation within the governing body are just two aspects of football that should (and could) be challenged if gender equity is to be achieved in the long term. Overhauling the women's game is not addressing those aspects of the football culture that position it as 'outside' of real football, and as already explained, is in fact perhaps enabling its continued exclusion.

The future

When placing the FAWSL within the wider context of European women's football, it is not alone in piloting experimental formats in order to increase the profile, competitiveness and commercial appeal of the game. In 2012, the BeNe League was launched, a pilot transnational league comprising the top women's teams from Belgium and the Netherlands (Prange, 2014). The league will be evaluated after three years, but there is concern that the Dutch teams are stronger than the Belgian teams, and that financial sustainability will be difficult to achieve. In Denmark and Sweden, a licensing system for female football clubs has been in place since 2012, representing a move towards professionalisation of the game in Scandinavia. However Kjær and Agergaard (2013) question whether this will be successful in a context where 'social cohesion and voluntarism provide an important rationale for clubs and soccer federations' (p. 829). This tension between discourses of participation and professionalisation continues to impact how women are positioned in the football sphere. Sustained evaluation of and reflection on developments in women's football across Europe is vital at such an unstable time for the sport.

The FA has released no information about their long-term strategy for the WSL. The Game Changer and FAWSL 2014–2018 documents discuss

DOI: 10.1057/9781137480323.0012

the current four-year cycle of the WSL that will end in 2018, but there is no public indication of their plans beyond then. Perhaps they do not know themselves what the long-term future entails for this experimental league.

Unifying the whole women's football pyramid is arguably the biggest challenge for the immediate future. As it currently stands, the summer and winter leagues are as distinct as they could be. They play oppositional schedules, there is a gulf in financial support and there is a real concern that if things remain as they are, the two pyramids will drift further apart. The two options for this are to revert to a winter game for the FAWSL (unlikely given the FA support for this summer scheduling) or gradually move the rest of the pyramid to a summer game (which will stretch limited resources even further). The only other outcome – maintaining the status quo – is perhaps the most likely but the least beneficial for the game as a whole as it can only widen the structural and cultural gulf between the two pyramids.

One thing that is clear is that the FA wants the WSL to be able to sustain itself financially, hence the reluctance to invest significant amounts. Documentation provided to help with 2014 applications stated that clubs should have a plan for future financial sustainability as the FA plan to 'taper or withdraw' funding by 2018 (The FA, 2013b).

Clubs are therefore expected to be able to maintain their current expenditure without FA assistance from 2018. Looking at the current situation across the two divisions, this might be easier for some than others. Clubs with strong financial backing from a male club – and not just any male club, but those in a strong financial position themselves, which excludes the majority – may find this easier than those who have less financial support and therefore have more reliance on the FA. It is hoped that clubs have secured external income from 'various revenue sources' such as commercial partnerships, but it is unlikely in reality that this will represent anything close to what a rich male professional football club might be able to provide. With no financial support from the FA, clubs who do not have this luxury will struggle to compete with those that do. Could this see a return to the late 1990s where teams with links to a male club – Arsenal, Charlton and Fulham – dominated the sport and others struggled to compete? Given what happened to two of these three when their male club decided to withdraw their funding (discussed in Chapter 3), this would be an uncomfortable step backwards for a sport that, at least for now, appears to be addressing the competitive imbalance

DOI: 10.1057/9781137480323.0012

that plagued it during the 2000s. Only time will tell whether this can remain now that the richer of the men's clubs have joined the party, and will want to see a return for their investment.

It will be interesting to monitor the future of the WSL to see if the withdrawal of funding by the FA is matched by a withdrawal of any degree of control. Currently the FA has ultimate control over the league and its clubs – they must comply with the FA regulations and as the Doncaster Belles case has proved, there is little space to challenge these. If they disagree with the licensing system, the summer league format, or any other aspect, clubs are welcome to leave the WSL. To be on the inside you have to buy into the WSL product, the culture and the structure. The FA are defining what the future of women's football will look like, what form it will take, and clubs and players have little or no influence on this. Chapter 4 discussed the inability of clubs or the groundswell of support to challenge this. Without the ability to challenge the status quo, female players and football clubs have no agency to make women's football what they think it should be.

Concluding remarks

This book reflects our critical thoughts on the FAWSL, from its con-ception through to the current status at the close of its fourth season. Criticism is healthy, and is vital for progression; the FA has the aim of increasing the profile of women's football, and if this is to succeed, it will bring with it increased scrutiny, and therefore criticism. As discussed earlier, critique cannot come from those who are within the FAWSL – compliance is the only way to maintain a position in the elite league. Some might argue that criticism is not what a league in its infancy needs; that the FA are doing an admirable job in their attempts to increase the profile of women's football in a sustainable way; or that instead of a critique, advice and recommendations would be of more use. We agree to some extent on all of the above. There is no doubt that the FAWSL has brought some benefits to women's football, the clubs involved and the players. But we would argue that because of the most visible aspects of the league – notably the club licensing system and the summer league format – any gains at this stage are purely superficial, and are doing little to elevate the position of women's football out of the inferior and marginalised status it has held throughout its development.

DOI: 10.1057/9781137480323.0012

Yet we do not profess to have any answers to the dilemma facing the sport. In promoting women's football as a sport in its own right, as different to the men's game – and celebrating those differences – it is likely to remain on the margin, 'outside' 'real' football. To some, this may not seem a problem. In fact it may be a benefit – professional men's football has its fair share of faults, and being fully integrated 'inside football', if this were to happen, would put the women's game at risk of the negative facets of men's football. There is already the concern with increased professionalism about an influx of foreign players, of money buying success and players moving clubs more frequently. But remaining on the periphery of football maintains the marginalisation of the female game. It is easy to dismiss it, to not take it seriously, to keep it off the radar. But what of the alternative? Women's football cannot compete with the established structure and culture of men's football, and it probably never will. Any media article written about women's football attracts comments about how the games are not as good, the players are not as good, and how the fact that people do not watch it in person or on television reinforces that perception. It needs to find its own space to develop. This is an argument for the summer league – a literal space in the football calendar for the women's game to occupy. Except this is not working, as the literal space it occupies is outside of what football is to many people, and the sport has not carved out a cultural space. This appears to be a no-win situation for women's football.

But this should not be the conclusion. Dominant discourses are only dominant because they are taken for granted at that moment in time. They are not totalising, and can therefore be challenged, and shift. Attitudes can change. What we do know is that the debate must continue. Questions must continue be asked about how women are to gain ground in what is possibly the strongest masculine domain in the UK. Academic critique must be used to keep the debate healthy, to keep discussions moving and to increase interest. The media also play a role, not just in increasing the profile of women's football (and other sports) but also in fostering debates, in encouraging people to think more deeply about women's football, to perhaps question their own preconceptions and understandings. What we do have right now, thanks to the FAWSL, is a platform upon which to push debates and start to challenge negative understandings. Without this platform, the football world will find it easier to ignore female participants, and this really would represent a step backwards.

DOI: 10.1057/9781137480323.0012

Notes

1 BBC3 is a digital channel aimed at bringing new content to 16–34-year-olds, with a smaller profile and viewing figures than the BBC's main channels, BBC1 and BBC2. This is evident in the fact that it is to become an online-only channel from 2015 (see BBC Trust, 2013).

2 Mike Newell, then Luton Town manager, was disciplined by the FA after making sexist comments about a female assistant referee. He is quoted as saying 'she should not be here. I know that sounds sexist, but I am sexist, so I am not going to be anything other than that. We have a problem in this country with political correctness, and bringing women into the game is not the way to improve refereeing and officialdom. It is absolutely beyond belief. When do we reach a stage when all officials are women, then we are in trouble. It is bad enough with the incapable referees and linesmen we have, but if you start bringing in women, you have big problems. It is tokenism, for the politically correct idiots' (http://www.theguardian.com/uk/2006/nov/12/football.gender). More recently, Sky Sports presenters Andy Gray and Richard Keys were removed from the air after making sexist comments about another female assistant referee. Their conversation included 'somebody better get down there and explain offside to her' *The Guardian*, http://www.telegraph.co.uk/sport/football/competitions/premier-league/8277518/Sky-Sports-presenters-Andy-Gray-and-Richard-Keys-say-sorry-after-mocking-lineswoman-during-Liverpool-victory.html.

3 http://www.sportengland.org/research/who-plays-sport/national-picture/.

4 http://www.womensfootball.eu/forum/index.php/topic,7865.0/wap2.html.

5 http://www.thefa.com/news/fawsl/2013/nov/new-league-structure-for-womens-game#47WwUpbCEAIGwFvW.99.

6 http://saveourwomenspremierleague.weebly.com/save-our-wpl.html details the campaign and protest.

7 See http://sportsandsensibility.blogspot.co.uk/2014/05/fas-game-changer-could-be-game-killer.html and http://www.telegraph.co.uk/sport/football/10487233/FA-faces-worthless-womens-football-revolt.html.

8 http://www.shekicks.net/news/view/9230.

9 http://www.fawsl.com/news/fa_wpl_to_get_entry_into_fa_wsl.html.

DOI: 10.1057/9781137480323.0012

References

Agergaard, S and Tiesler, N C (eds) (2014). *Women, Soccer and Transnational Migration.* London: Routledge.

Aoki, K, Crumbach, S, Naicker, C, Schmitter, S and Smith, N (2010). *Identifying Best Practice in Women's Football – Case Study in the European Context.* FIFA Master 10th Edition. Available online at http://www.cies-uni.org/ sites/default/files/identifying_best_practices_in_ women_football.pdf.

Ashdown, J and Gibson, O (2011). BBC makes U-turn on England Women's World Cup quarter-final. *The Guardian,* 8 July 2011. Available online at: http:// www.theguardian.com/football/2011/jul/08/bbc- england-women-world-cup.

Bayle, E, Jaccard, E and Philippe, V (2013). Synergies football masculin et féminin: vers un nouveau modèle stratégique pour les clubs professionnels européens? *Revue Européenne de Management du sport,* 39, 1–25.

BBC (2013). Lincoln Ladies: Move to Nottingham branded 'own goal'. *The BBC online,* 29 April 2013. Available online at: http://www.bbc.co.uk/news/ uk-england-lincolnshire-22335404.

BBC Sport (2006). Terry named new England skipper. *BBC SPORT Online,* 10 August 2006. Available online at: http://news.bbc.co.uk/go/pr/fr/-/sport1/hi/football/ internationals/4780745.stm.

BBC Sport (2011). WSL progress continuing, says Liverpool's Vicky Jones. *BBC Sport online,* 15 June 2011. Available online at: http://www.bbc.co.uk/sport/0/ football/13762946.

DOI: 10.1057/9781137480323.0013

BBC Trust (2013). *BBC3 Service Licence*. Issued September 2013.

Bell, B (2012) Levelling the playing field? Post-Euro 2005 development of women's football in the north-west of England. *Sport in Society: Cultures, Commerce, Media, Politics*, 15/3, 349–368.

Bell, B and Blakey, P (2010). Do boys and girls go out to play? Women's football and social marketing at Euro 2005. *International Journal of Sport Management and Marketing*, 7/3–4, 156–172.

Caudwell, J (1999). Women's football in the United Kingdom: Theorising gender and unpacking the butch lesbian image. *Journal of Sport and Social Issues*, 23/4, 390–402.

Caudwell, J (2003). Sporting gender: Women's footballing bodies as sites/sights for the [re]articulation of sex, gender and desire. *Sociology of Sport Journal*, 20, 371–386.

Caudwell, J (2004). Out on the field of play: Women's experiences of gender and sexuality in football contexts. In S Wagg (ed.) *British Football and Social Exclusion*. London: Routledge.

Christenson, M and Kelso, P (2004). Soccer chief's plan to boost women's game? Hotpants. *The Guardian*, 16 January 2004. Available online at: http://www.theguardian.com/uk/2004/jan/16/football.gender.

Cloake, M (2013). What the scandal of Doncaster Belles tells us about modern football. *The New Statesman*, 30 May 2013. Available online at: http://www.newstatesman.com/business/2013/05/what-scandal-doncaster-belles-tells-us-about-modern-football.

Conn, D (2011). Women's Super League aims to step out of men's shadow. *The Guardian*, 7 April 2011. Available online at: http://www.theguardian.com/football/blog/2011/apr/07/womens-super-league-launch.

Crosset, T (1995). *Outsiders in the Clubhouse: The World of Women's Professional Golf*. Albany: State University of New York Press.

De varona, D (2003). 'M's' in football: Myths, management, marketing, media and money. A reprise. *Soccer and Society*, 4/2–3, 7–13.

Department for Culture, Media and Sport (DCMS) (2006). *Women's Football: Fourth Report of Session 2005–06*. London: The Stationary Office.

Department for Culture, Media and Sport (DCMS) (2011). *Football Governance: Seventh Report of Session 2010–12*. London: The Stationary Office.

Department for Culture, Media and Sport (DCMS) (2013). *Football Governance Follow-Up: Fourth Report of Session 2012–13*. London: The Stationary Office.

DOI: 10.1057/9781137480323.0013

Department for Culture, Media and Sport (DCMS) (2014). *Women and Sport: First Report of Session 2014–2015*. London: The Stationary Office.

Dixon, R (2011). Women's football is ahead of the game. *The Guardian*, 18 July 2011. Available online at: http://www.theguardian.com/commentisfree/2011/jul/18/womens-football-world-cup.

Dunmore, T (2009). The Women's Premier League to kick off under a cloud. *PitchInvasion.net*, 15 August 2009. Available online at: http://pitchinvasion.net/blog/2009/08/15/the-womens-premier-league-to-kick-off-under-a- cloud/.

Fasting, K (2004). Small country – big results. In F Hong and J A Mangan (eds) *Soccer, Women, Sexual Liberation: Kicking Off a New Era*. London: Routledge, pp. 190–213.

Fielding-Lloyd, B and Meân, L (2011). 'I don't think I can catch it': Women, confidence and responsibility in football coach education. *Soccer and Society*, 12/3, 345–364.

Forbes, A, Edwards, L and Fleming, S (2014). 'Women can't referee': Exploring the experiences of female football officials within UK football culture. *Soccer and Society*, published online 6 February 2014.

The Football Association (2001). *The Football Development Strategy 2001–2006*. London: Football Association.

The Football Association (2005). *FA Structural Review*. London: The Football Association.

The Football Association (2008). *Women's and Girls Football Strategy: Championing Growth and Excellence*. Available online at: http://nav.thefa.com/sitecore/content/TheFA/Home/GetIntoFootball/Players/PlayersPages/WomensAndGirls/~/media/Files/PDF/TheFA/WomensStrategy.ashx/WomensStrategy.pdf.

The Football Association (2009a). Clubs Hear Plans for Super League. *TheFA.com*, 30 October 2009. Available online at: http://nav.thefa.com/sitecore/content/TheFA/Home/Leagues/SuperLeague/NewsAndFeatures/2009/WSLMeetingWatmore.

The Football Association (2009b). *Be Part of Football's Future. The FA Women's Super League, Launching in 2011*. London: The Football Association.

The Football Association (2010). *Frequently Asked Questions on The FA WSL*. London: The Football Association.

The Football Association (2012a). *Game Changer: The FA Plan for Women's Football in England 2013–2018*. London: The Football Association.

DOI: 10.1057/9781137480323.0013

The Football Association (2012b). *Report and Financial Statements*, 31 December 2012. London: The Football Association.

The Football Association (2012c). *Frequently Asked Questions on The FA WSL*. London: The Football Association.

The Football Association (2013a). *The FA Women's Super League 2014–2018*. London: The Football Association.

The Football Association (2013b). *February Updates for FA WSL Applications*. *Thefa.com*. Available online at http://t.co/kuLZY9JyCo.

The Football Association (2013c). Decision and reasons of the independent appeals panel; Doncaster Rovers Belles Ladies Football Club and the Football Association. *Thefa.com*. Available online at: http://www.thefa.com/News/governance/2013/jun/doncaster-belles-appeal-statement.aspx.

The Football Association Women's Super League (FAWSL) (2013). *Frequently Asked Questions*. *Thefa.com*. Available online at: http://www.fawsl.com/news/faqs_1_to_5.html.

Galtung, J and Ruge, M (1965). The structure of foreign news: The presentation of the Congo, Cuba and Cyprus crises in four Norwegian newspapers. Journal of Peace Research, 2, 64–91.

Gayle, D (2012). Fury from fans as 'sexist' Sky Sports cuts short women's FA Cup Final coverage – robbing viewers of the result. *The Daily Mail*, 29 May 2012. Available online at: http://www.dailymail.co.uk/news/article-2151446/Fury-fans-sexist-Sky-Sports-cuts-short-womens-FA-Cup-Final-coverage--robbing-viewers-result.html.

Gibson, O (2012). FA unveils bold plan to make women's football England's second sport. *The Guardian*, 24 October 2012. Available online at: http://www.theguardian.com/football/2012/oct/24/fa-womens-football-england.

Gibson, O (2014). Sport England's £1.6m cut to FA 'a warning over grassroots failure'. *The Guardian*, 27 March 2014. Available online at: http://www.theguardian.com/football/2014/mar/27/sport-england-funding-cut-fa-warning-grassroots-golf-netball-hockey-rowing.

Griggs, G. (2004). Are boys just 'hogging the ball'?: An examination of the factors that influence primary school girls' participation in football. *Bulletin of Physical Education*, 40/2, 161–177.

Griggs, G and Biscomb, K (2010). Theresa Bennett is 42 ... but what's new? *Soccer and Society*, 11/5, 668–676.

Giulianotti, R (1999). *Football: A Sociology of the Global Game*. Oxford: Polity Press.

DOI: 10.1057/9781137480323.0013

Guardian (2013). 'The corrections column co-editor on … women's sport in *The Guardian*'. Available online at: http://www.theguardian. com/commentisfree/2013/mar/10/womens-sport-guardian-coverage.

Hamil, S, Walters, G and Watson, L (2010). The model of governance at FC Barcelona: Balancing member democracy, commercial strategy, corporate social responsibility and sporting performance, *Soccer and Society*, 11/4, 475–504.

Harris, J (2001). Playing the man's game: Sites of resistance and incorporation in women's football. *World Leisure*, 43/4, 22–29.

Harris, J (2002). 'No you can't play, you're a girl': Some primary school recollections of female football players. *The Bulletin of Physical Education*, 38/3, 161–178.

Harris, J (1999). Lie back and think of England: The women of Euro 96. *Journal of Sport and Social Issues* 23/2, 96–110.

Harris, J. (2007). Doing gender on and off the pitch: The world of female football players. *Sociological Research Online*, 12/1. Available online at: http://www.socresonline.org.uk/12/1/harris.html.

Harlow, P (2005). FA hails Euro 2005 as big success. *BBC Sport*, Monday, 13 June 2005. Accessed at http://news.bbc.co.uk/sport1/hi/football/women/4087208.stm.

Hjelm, J and Olofsson, E (2004). A breakthrough: Women's football in Sweden. In F Hong and J A Mangan (eds) *Soccer, Women, Sexual Liberation: Kicking Off a New Era*. London: Routledge, pp. 190–213.

Hong, F and Mangan, J A (eds) (2004). *Soccer, Women, Sexual Liberation: Kicking Off a New Era*. London: Routledge, pp. 190–213.

James, D (2007). China events have got us boys talking about the girls. *The Observer*, 16 September 2007. Available online at: http://football.guardian.co.uk/comments/story/0,,2170132,00.html. First accessed 18 September 2007.

Jeanes, R and Kay, T (2007). Can football be a female game? An examination of girls' perceptions of football and gender identity, in J Magee, J Caudwell, K Liston and S Scraton (eds) *Women, Football and Europe: Histories, Equity and Experiences*. Oxford: Meyer and Meyer Sport Ltd.

Joyce, M (2006). Wimbledon FC – No to Merton! In Brimson, D (ed.) *Rebellion: The Inside Story of Football's Protest Movement*. London: John Blake.

DOI: 10.1057/9781137480323.0013

Kearney, M C (2011). Tough girls in a rough game: Televising the unruly female athletes of contemporary roller derby. *Feminist Media Studies*, 11/3, 283–301.

Kessel, A (2008). The invincibles. *The Observer*, 4 May, 2008. Available online at: http://www.theguardian.com/football/2008/may/04/sportfeatures.gender.

Kessel, A (2010). FA invests £3m in eight-club elite league for women. *The Guardian*, 16 December 2010. Available online at: http://www.theguardian.com/football/2010/dec/16/new-womens-league.

King, B (2009). Confident, yes, but can new league survive? *SportsBusiness Journal*, 2 March 2009. Available online at: http://www.sportsbusinessdaily.com/Journal/Issues/2009/03/20090302/SBJ-In-Depth/Confident-Yes-But-Can-New-League-Survive.aspx.

Kjær, J B and Agergaard, S (2013). Understanding women's professional soccer: The case of Denmark and Sweden. *Soccer and Society*, 14/6, 816–833.

Leighton, T (2007a). Charlton shut down women's team. BBC Sport, 23 June 2007. Available online at: http://news.bbc.co.uk/sport1/hi/football/women/6233506.stm.

Leighton, T (2007b). Sports minister calls for England support. *The Guardian*, 12 November 2007. Available online at: http://www.theguardian.com/football/2007/nov/12/womensfootball.sport.

Leighton, T (2009a). Anger at delay of women's summer Super League. *The Guardian*, 6 April 2009. Available at: http://www.theguardian.com/football/2009/apr/06/womens-football-super-league-fa.

Leighton, T (2009b). England's Helsinki heroics put Super League back on track for 2011. *The Guardian*, 12 September 2009. Available online at: http://www.theguardian.com/football/2009/sep/11/england-women-european-championship-super-league.

Leighton, T (2010a). Lianne Sanderson cites Super League delay as reason for US move. *The Guardian*, 24 January 2010. Available online at: http://www.theguardian.com/football/2010/jan/24/womens-football-lianne-sanderson.

Leighton, T (2010b). Lincoln City the surprise name in newly formed Women's Super League. *The Guardian*, 21 March 2010. Available online at: http://www.theguardian.com/football/2010/mar/21/women-football-super-league.

Leighton, T (2010c). Leeds women kick off defence of Premier League Cup in United guise. *The Guardian*, 29 August 2010. Available

DOI: 10.1057/9781137480323.0013

online at: http://www.theguardian.com/football/2010/aug/29/leeds-sunderland-premier-league-cup.

Leighton, T (2011a). Nottingham Forest women's team may fold before cup final. *The Guardian*, 13 February 2011. Available online at: http://www.theguardian.com/football/2011/feb/13/nottingham-forest-womens-football.

Leighton, T (2011b). Arsenal face fixture pile-up as inaugural Women's Super League begins. *The Guardian*, 10 April 2011. Available online at: http://www.theguardian.com/football/2011/apr/10/arsenal-chelsea-women-super-league.

Leighton, T (2011c). Blackburn's women relegated after decision to snub Super League. *The Guardian*, 1 May 2011. Available online at http://www.theguardian.com/football/2011/may/01/blackburn-rovers-womens-football.

Leighton, T (2011d). Super League has helped England women's World Cup plans, says coach. *The Guardian*, 15 May 2011. Available online at: http://www.theguardian.com/football/2011/may/15/super-league-england-hope-powell.

Leighton, T (2011e). Women's Premier League kicks off – but will the winners get promotion? *The Guardian*, 21 August 2011. Available online at: http://www.theguardian.com/football/2011/aug/21/womens-premier-league.

Lincolnshire Echo (2013). Lincoln Ladies: 'Supporters will not follow the club to Nottingham'. *The Lincolnshire Echo*, 2 May 2013. Available online at: http://www.lincolnshireecho.co.uk/Lincoln-Ladies-Supporters-follow-club-Nottingham/story-18867225-detail/story.html#axzz2eP2ax99o.

Lopez, S (1997). *Women on the Ball*. London: Scarlet Press.

Macerskill, S (2011). Sky Sports presenters Andy Gray and Richard Keys say sorry after mocking lineswoman during Liverpool victory. *The Telegraph*, 23 January 2011. Available online at: http://www.telegraph.co.uk/sport/football/competitions/premier-league/8277518/Sky-Sports-presenters-Andy-Gray-and-Richard-Keys-say-sorry-after-mocking-lineswoman-during-Liverpool-victory.html.

Magowan, (2013). Lincoln Ladies: Casey Stoney accepts fans' anger over move. *BBC Sport online*, 3 May 2013. Available online at: http://www.bbc.co.uk/sport/0/football/22369525.

Martin, Adam and McDonald, Mary G (2012). Covering women's sport? An analysis of Sports Illustrated covers from 1987–2009 and ESPN the magazine covers from 1998–2009. *Graduate Journal of Sport, Exercise & Physical Education Research*, 1, 81–97.

Martinez, D P (2008). Soccer in the USA: 'holding out for a hero'? *Soccer and Society*, 9/2, 231–243.

Melling, A (1999). 'Plucky Lasses', 'Pea Soup' and Politics: The role of ladies football during the 1921 miners' lock-out in Wigan and Leigh. *The International Journal of the History of Sport* 16/1, 38–64.

The Metro (2013). Casey Stoney hails Olympic effect on women's football ahead of new FA Women's Super League season. Available online at: http://metro.co.uk/2013/03/17/casey-stoney-hails-olympic-effect-on-womens-football-ahead-of-new-fa-womens-super-league-season-3545267/.

The Mirror (2012). An antidote to fakery: Why Jessica Ennis is the role model we need for our girls. 8 August 2012. Available online at: http://www.mirror.co.uk/news/uk-news/jessica-ennis-is-the-role-model-we-need-1233368.

Murray, D and Howatt, G (2009). The 'enrichment hypothesis' as an explanation of women's participation in rugby. *Annals of Leisure Research*, 12/1, 65–82.

Newsham, G J (1997). *In a League of Their Own! The Dick, Kerr Ladies Football Club*. London: Scarlet Press.

Norman, L (2014). A crisis of confidence: women coaches' responses to their engagement in resistance, *Sport, Education and Society*, 19/5, 532–551.

Oatley, J (2009). Women's game deserves better. *BBC Sport*. Available online at: http://www.bbc.co.uk/blogs/legacy/jacquioatley/2009/04/women_footballers_deserve_bett.html.

Pfister, G (2004). The challenges of women's football in East and West Germany: A comparative study. In Fan Hong and J A Mangan (eds) *Soccer, Women, Sexual Liberation: Kicking Off a New Era*. London: Routledge, pp. 190–213.

Pfister, G, Fasting, K, Scraton, S and Vasquez, B (2002). Women and football – a contradiction? The beginnings of women's football in four European countries. In S. Scraton and A. Flintoff (eds) *Gender and Sport: A Reader*. London: Routledge.

Popular Stand (2013), 'The Belles' Toll; on the FA's relegation of the Doncaster Belles', 13 May 2013. Available online at: http://popularstand.wordpress.com/2013/05/13/the-belles-toll-on-the-fas-relegation-of-the-doncaster-belles.

DOI: 10.1057/9781137480323.0013

Popular Stand (2013), 'The Belles' Toll; update and points of action', 16 May 2013, Available online at: http://popularstand.wordpress.com/2013/05/16/the-belles-toll-update-and-points-of-action.

Popular Stand (2013), 'Silenced Belles; on the FA's rejection of the Doncaster Belles' appeal', 29 June 2013. Available online at: http://popularstand.wordpress.com/2013/06/29/silenced-belles-on-the-fas-rejection-of-the-doncaster-belles-appeal.

Prange, M (2014). Changing the Landscape of European Football: Women football's transformative effect on Europe's public sphere analysed by way of the transnational BeNe League case. Paper presented at *From Habermas to Fanblogs: Exploring the Public Sphere of European Football* Conference, Middle Eastern Technical University, Ankara, April 2014.

The Premier League (2014). Manchester City Women's football show dedication to community. *The Premier League website*, 30 January 2014. Available online at: http://www.premierleague.com/en-gb/news/news/2013-14/jan/manchester-city-womens-launch-with-commitment-to-community.html.

The Press Association (2011). Andy Burnham urges BBC to show England women's World Cup quarter. *The Guardian*, 8 July 2011. Available online at: http://www.theguardian.com/football/2011/jul/08/andy-burnham-england-womens-world-cup.

Prudhomme- Poncet, L (2007). Les femmes, balle au pied: A history of French women's football. In J Magee, J Caudwell, K Liston and S Scraton (eds) *Women, Football and Europe: History, Equalities and Experience*, vol. 1. Oxford: Meyer and Meyer Sport Ltd, pp. 27–40.

Riach, (2013). Lincoln Ladies' rebirth as Notts County sparks new franchise fury. *The Guardian*, 2 May 2013. Available online at: http://www.theguardian.com/football/2013/may/02/lincoln-ladies-notts-county-fans.

Ronay, B (2011). Women's Super League opens with less than pitch perfect display. *The Guardian*, 13 April 2011. Available online at: http://www.theguardian.com/football/2011/apr/13/womens-super-league-arsenal-chelsea.

Schulz, W F (1982). News structure and people's awareness of political events. *International Communication Gazette*, 30: 139–153.

Scraton, S, Caudwell, J and Holland, S (2005). 'Bend it like Patel': Centring 'race', ethnicity and gender in feminist analysis of women's football in England. *International Review for the Sociology of Sport*, 40/1, 71–88.

DOI: 10.1057/9781137480323.0013

Scraton, S, Fasting, K, Pfister, G and Bunual, A (1999). It's still a man's game? The experiences of top-level European women footballers. *International Review for the Sociology of Sport*, 34/2, 99–111.

Semyonov, M (1981). Changing roles of women: Participation in Olympic Games. *Social Science Quarterly*, 62/4, 735–743.

Senaux, B (2011). The regulated commercialisation of French football. In H. Gammelsæter and B. Senaux (eds) *The Organisation and Governance of Top Football across Europe*. London: Routledge.

Skelton, C (2000). A passion for football: Dominant masculinities and primary schooling. *Sport, Education and Society*, 5/1, 5–18.

Skille, E A (2008). Biggest but smallest: Female football and the case of Norway. *Soccer and Society*, 9/4, 520–531.

Stylist (2012). 'Foul play: Why is there sexism in sport?' Available online at: http://www.stylist.co.uk/people/foul-play-why-is-there-sexism-in-sport.

Sugden, J and Tomlinson, A (1994). Soccer culture, national identity, and the World Cup. In J Sugden and A Tomlinson (eds) *Hosts and Champions: Soccer Cultures, National Identities and the USA World Cup*. Aldershot: Arena.

Tate, T (2013). *Girls with Balls: The Secret History of Women's Football*. London: John Blake Publishing Ltd.

The Telegraph (2012), London 2012 Olympics: Record crowd watches Team GB women beat Brazil to reach quarter-finals, *The Telegraph*, 1 August 2012.

This is Lincolnshire (2013). Lincoln Ladies to become Notts County Ladies from 2014. *This is Lincolnshire online*, 26 April 2013. Available online at: http://www.thisislincolnshire.co.uk/Lincoln-Ladies-Notts-County-Ladies-2014/story-18814461-detail/story.html#axzz2eP2ax99o.

Thorne and District Gazette (2013). Arsenal's Akers backs the Belles, 29 May 2013. Available online at: http://www.thornegazette.co.uk/sport/local-sport/doncaster-belles-arsenal-s-akers-backs-the-belles-1-5718732.

Twohundredpercent (2013). The FA's betrayal of Doncaster Rovers Belles, 16 May 2013. Available online at: http://twohundredpercent.net/?p=23089.

Welford, J (2008). *What's the Score? Women in Football in England*. Unpublished PhD thesis, Loughborough University.

Welford, J (2011). Tokenism, Ties and Talking too Loudly: Women's experiences in

DOI: 10.1057/9781137480323.0013

non-playing football roles. *Soccer and Society,* 12/3, 365–381.

Welford, J (2013). Outsiders on the Inside: Integrating female and male football clubs in the UK. Paper presented at *Women's Football: Played, Watched, Talked about* conference, University of Copenhagen, June 2013.

Welford, J and Kay, T (2007). Negotiating barriers to entering and participating in football: Strategies employed by female footballers in the United Kingdom, in *Women, Football and Europe: Histories, Equity and Experiences,* (eds) J Magee, J Caudwell, K Liston and S Scraton, Oxford: Meyer and Meyer Sport Ltd, pp. 151–172.

When Saturday Comes (2013a). Women's football still shunned by national media. *WSC online,* 11 July 2013. Available online at: http://www.wsc.co.uk/wsc-daily/1164-july-2013/10046-women-s-football-still-being-shunned-by-national-media.

When Saturday Comes (2013b). FA try to silence Doncaster Belles cup final protest. *WSC online,* 28 May 2013. Available online at: http://www.wsc.co.uk/wsc-daily/1162-may-2013/9843-fa-try-to-silence-doncaster-belles-cup-final-protest.

Williams, Jean (2003). *A Game for Rough Girls? A History of Women's Football in Britain.* London: Routledge.

Williams, Jean (2004). The fastest growing sport? Women and football in England. In F Hong and J A Mangan (eds) *Soccer, Women, Sexual Liberation: Kicking Off a New Era.* London: Frank Cass.

Williams, Jean (2006). An equality too far? Historical and contemporary perspectives of gender inequality in British and international football. *Historical Social Research,* 31/1: 151–169.

Williams, Jean (2007). *A Beautiful Game: International Perspectives on Women's Football.* New York: Berg.

Williams, Jean (2013). *Globalising Women's Football: Europe, Migration and Professionalization.* Bern: Peter Lang.

Williams, John and Woodhouse, J (1991). Can play, will play? Women and football in Britain. In J Williams and S Wagg (eds) *British Football and Social Change: Getting into Europe.* Leicester University Press.

Williamson, D J (1991). *Belles of the Ball.* Devon: R&D Associates.

Williamson, L (2013). Doncaster Belles have been betrayed by the FA. *The Daily Mail,* 22 June 2013. Available online at: http://www.dailymail.co.uk/sport/article-2346937/Doncaster-Belles-betrayed-FA--Laura-Williamson.html.

DOI: 10.1057/9781137480323.0013

Women's Sport and Fitness Foundation (WSFF) (2008). *Women in Sport Audit*. Available online at: http://www.cwsportspartnership.org/files/wsff_sport_audit.pdf 25 June 2014.

Women's Sport and Fitness Foundation (WSFF) (2009). *Prime Time: The Case for Commercial Investment in Women's Sport*. London.

Women's Sport and Fitness Foundation (WSFF) (2011). *Big Deal? 2011: The Case for Commercial Investment in Women's Sport*. London.

Women's Sport and Fitness Foundation (WSFF) (2014). *Women's Sport: Say Yes to Success*. London.

DOI: 10.1057/9781137480323.0013

Index

DOI: 10.1057/9781137480323.0014

DOI: 10.1057/9781137480323.0014